Adult Bible St[

Summer 2021 • Vol. 28,

Editorial and Design Team
  Jan Turrentine, Editor
  Tonya Williams, Production Editor
  Ken Strickland, Designer

Administrative Team
  Rev. Brian K. Milford,
    President and Publisher
  Marjorie M. Pon, Associate Publisher
and Editor, Church School Publications

ADULT BIBLE STUDIES (ISSN 0149-8347): An official resource for The United Methodist Church approved by the General Board of Discipleship and published quarterly by Cokesbury, The United Methodist Publishing House, 2222 Rosa L. Parks Blvd., Nashville, Tennessee 37228. Copyright © 2021 by Cokesbury. Send address changes to ADULT BIBLE STUDIES, 2222 Rosa L. Parks Blvd., Nashville, Tennessee 37228.

To order copies of this publication, call toll free: **800-672-1789**. FAX your order to **800-445-8189**. Telecommunications Device for the Deaf/Telex Telephone: **800-227-4091**. Automated order system is available after office hours. Or order through Cokesbury.com. Use your Cokesbury account, American Express, Visa, Discover, or Mastercard.

For permission to reproduce any material in this publication, call 615-749-6268, or write to Permissions Office, 2222 Rosa L. Parks Blvd., Nashville, Tennessee 37228. Scripture quotations in this publication, unless otherwise indicated, are from the Common English Bible, copyright 2011. Used by permission.

ADULT BIBLE STUDIES is designed to help adults understand the meaning and authority of the Bible for Christian life. Daily study helps are published in *Daily Bible Study*. Leadership helps are published in *Adult Bible Studies Teacher* and at AdultBibleStudies.com.

Cover photo: Shutterstock

Michelle Morris

Michelle J. Morris is currently serving as lead equipper for the Center for Vitality in the Arkansas Conference of The United Methodist Church.

Michelle has a BA in English and French and an MA in Comparative Literature from the University of Arkansas. She graduated with an MDiv from Perkins School of Theology in 2009 and a PhD from the Graduate Program in Religious Studies at Southern Methodist University in 2014. She also graduated with a certificate in Women's and Gender Studies. Her dissertation examined the subject of infertility in the New Testament.

She and her husband, Travis, have a son, Soren (not named for Kierkegaard).

Adult Bible Studies is available to **readers with visual challenges** through BookShare.org. To use BookShare.org, persons must have certified disabilities and must become members of the site. Churches can purchase memberships on behalf of their member(s) who need the service. There is a small one-time setup fee, plus a modest annual membership fee. At the website, files are converted to computerized audio for download to CD or iPod, as well as to other audio devices (such as DAISY format). Braille is also available, as are other options. Once individuals have a membership, they have access to thousands of titles in addition to *ABS*. Live-narrated audio for persons with certified disabilities is available from AUDIOBOOK MINISTRIES at http://www.audiobookministries.org/.

Contents

Respond

"Okay, just calm down now. It can't be all that bad."

"Everything happens for a reason. You'll see."

"It's time to move on now. You'll eventually get over this."

"Well, I really think you should just [insert 'helpful' suggestion here]."

We could all probably pick a line and acknowledge that we've heard it or something equally unhelpful at the worst possible time in our lives. Most everyone who says things like these means to be supportive. But the truth is, "advice" like this isn't supportive because it suggests that what the other person is feeling is inappropriate or invalid. It also implies that the one offering the advice is wiser and knows oh so much better.

Just ask Job. There he sat—innocent, grieving, despairing, disgraced—while his wife encouraged him to "curse God, and die" (Job 2:9). His friends, seeing his deep pain, went to "console and comfort him" (verse 11) and managed to keep their mouths shut for a full week, but they eventually accused him of unconfessed sin that caused all his trouble. Job had some pretty strong words for God, and God kept quiet and let him speak. But eventually, it was God's turn, and God made sure Job understood to whom he was speaking.

We may have had similar conversations with God, or at least come close. What Job discovered, and what Joseph—sold into slavery by his jealous brothers—discovered before him is this: God never stops being God. God is always present, always gracious, always loving. God is God, and that is enough. God is always enough.

Our lessons this quarter, written by Michelle Morris, remind us that, even when we cannot discern it, God is at work behind the scenes. Despite how desperate our circumstances might seem, God always has the last word. The last word, as Joseph and Job discovered, is never suffering. The last word is hope. And that is a word our neighbors, the people next door and those around the world, need to hear.

Jan Turrentine

Jan Turrentine
AdultBibleStudies@cokesbury.com

Daily Bible Readings (Unit 1)

May 31
Psalm 37:1-15

June 1
Genesis 37:1-11

June 2
Genesis 37:12-22

June 3
Genesis 37:23-30

June 4
Psalm 31:9-13

June 5
Genesis 37:31-38

June 6
Deuteronomy 33:13-17

June 7
Psalm 1:1-6

June 8
Genesis 39:1-6

June 9
Genesis 39:6-20

June 10
Proverbs 6:20-26

June 11
Genesis 39:20-23

June 12
Genesis 40:1-15, 23

June 13
Genesis 40:16-22

June 14
Genesis 41:1-16

June 15
Genesis 41:17-32

June 16
Genesis 41:33-45

June 17
Genesis 41:46-57

June 18
Genesis 47:27-31

June 19
Genesis 49:22-26, 28

June 20
Acts 7:9-16

June 21
Genesis 42:1-24

June 22
Genesis 43:1-34

June 23
Genesis 44:1-17

June 24
Genesis 44:18-34

June 25
Genesis 45:1-15

June 26
Genesis 45:16-28

June 27
Psalm 105:16-23

Unit 1
Intended for Good

My mentor once shared that some of the people he was mentoring had trouble defining *grace*. They had vague ideas but nothing they could succinctly put into words. *Grace* is God's loving presence in our lives. It is that simple and that profound. It is hard to articulate sometimes, but when we experience it, it is as clear as a cloudless sky.

John Wesley saw grace as a lifelong journey of walking with God. That journey begins even before we are aware that is where we are walking. Wesley defined three principle stages in that journey:

Prevenient grace, the grace extended to us before we know we need a relationship with God. It is how God woos us into that loving relationship. *Prevenient* means "to go before." It is all the ways God goes before us to show us what a life with God is like.

Justifying grace, the point at which we come to recognize how much God loves us and desires to walk with us and we turn and accept that love. It is that realization of how much we need God, and we seek the salvation extended to us by Jesus Christ. And seeing God love us so much as to face death to bring us life is heartbreaking and profoundly compelling. We confess and humbly receive that gift freely given by Jesus and experience the power of justifying grace.

Sanctifying grace, the life we live seeking to love more like Christ. If we all died right at the moment of justification, our journey in grace would have adequately ceased. However, since the vast majority of us have life to live past that moment, we live in sanctifying grace. The Holy Spirit guides and nurtures us into being the people of God, closer each day to being perfected in the love of Jesus.

God's grace was at work behind the scenes in the life of Joseph and his brothers. As we look at Joseph's story over this quarter, we get a better understanding of the wonderful gift of God's grace.

Focal Passage: Genesis 37:5-28
Background Text: Genesis 37:1-36
Purpose Statement: To affirm that we all need God's grace

Genesis 37:5-28

⁵Joseph had a dream and told it to his brothers, which made them hate him even more. ⁶He said to them, "Listen to this dream I had. ⁷When we were binding stalks of grain in the field, my stalk got up and stood upright, while your stalks gathered around it and bowed down to my stalk."

⁸His brothers said to him, "Will you really be our king and rule over us?" So they hated him even more because of the dreams he told them.

⁹Then Joseph had another dream and described it to his brothers: "I've just dreamed again, and this time the sun and the moon and eleven stars were bowing down to me."

¹⁰When he described it to his father and brothers, his father scolded him and said to him, "What kind of dreams have you dreamed? Am I and your mother and your brothers supposed to come and bow down to the ground in front of you?" ¹¹His brothers were jealous of him, but his father took careful note of the matter.

¹²Joseph's brothers went to tend their father's flocks near Shechem. ¹³Israel said to Joseph, "Aren't your

brothers tending the sheep near Shechem? Come, I'll send you to them."

And he said, "I'm ready."

¹⁴Jacob said to him, "Go! Find out how your brothers are and how the flock is, and report back to me."

So Jacob sent him from the Hebron Valley. When he approached Shechem, ¹⁵a man found him wandering in the field and asked him, "What are you looking for?"

¹⁶Joseph said, "I'm looking for my brothers. Tell me, where are they tending the sheep?"

¹⁷The man said, "They left here. I heard them saying, 'Let's go to Dothan.'" So Joseph went after his brothers and found them in Dothan.

¹⁸They saw Joseph in the distance before he got close to them, and they plotted to kill him. ¹⁹The brothers said to each other, "Here comes the big dreamer. ²⁰Come on now, let's kill him and throw him into one of the cisterns, and we'll say a wild animal devoured him. Then we will see what becomes of his dreams!"

²¹When Reuben heard what they said, he saved him from them, telling them, "Let's not take his life." ²²Reuben said to them, "Don't spill his blood! Throw him into this desert cistern, but don't lay a hand on him." He intended to save Joseph from them and take him back to his father.

²³When Joseph reached his brothers, they stripped off Joseph's long robe, ²⁴took him, and threw him into the

cistern, an empty cistern with no water in it. ²⁵When they sat down to eat, they looked up and saw a caravan of Ishmaelites coming from Gilead, with camels carrying sweet resin, medicinal resin, and fragrant resin on their way down to Egypt. ²⁶Judah said to his brothers, "What do we gain if we kill our brother and hide his blood? ²⁷Come on, let's sell him to the Ishmaelites. Let's not harm him because he's our brother; he's family." His brothers agreed. ²⁸When some Midianite traders passed by, they pulled Joseph up out of the cistern. They sold him to the Ishmaelites for twenty pieces of silver, and they brought Joseph to Egypt.

Key Verses: "What do we gain if we kill our brother and hide his blood? Come on, let's sell him to the Ishmaelites. Let's not harm him because he's our brother; he's family" (Genesis 37:26-27).

My mom was one of 21 brothers and sisters. I will pause a moment while you pull your jaw off the floor. When I drop that one detail into a conversation, it stops everything. People have a lot of questions. You probably do, too, so let me fill in the gaps.

Yes, they were all blood-related to her but not necessarily to one another. Some were her dad's kids, and some were her mom's. There was also an age difference of just over 20 years between my grandpa and grandma, so my mom had siblings who were older than her mother. It was an interesting family tree.

It also meant, with so many people, that a feud was usually going on. That was especially the case as those brothers and sisters had children and those children had children. With the increase in people came the increase in the likelihood of conflict.

The funny thing is, I know that my mom's family fought. I know there were betrayals and battles. I know there were times when people weren't speaking to one another, sometimes for years. But as I sit here, I can't think of any instances that didn't eventually experience reconciliation. It strikes me that, even in the most difficult situations, there was room for forgiveness. There was the possibility for reconciliation. After all, it wasn't like any one of them sold another one into slavery!

The stretch of Genesis in which our text falls is called "the Joseph novella." It is a short but dramatic telling of a family that knew brokenness and loss. But ultimately, through God's redemptive grace, they knew healing for themselves and salvation for whole nations. The road to get there, however, was more than a little bumpy.

He's Our Brother, but . . .

My parents would sometimes sing a song, the only line of which I remember is "He ain't heavy. He's my brother." I have no idea what that line means. I do remember, though, that my dad usually broke into that line when he was frustrated with something to do with family. I am not sure if the line was his way of expressing that frustration or if he had to remind himself that family is family, no matter what.

I wonder if Joseph's brothers had a song like that, a song that came to their minds when this one who always seemed to be favored (firstborn to the favorite wife, recipient of the special coat) took the opportunity to remind them just how favored he was, like when Joseph shared his dream (Genesis 37:5-7). It is funny that, in this Joseph saga, his ability to interpret dreams was so needed and admired. These dreams seem pretty obvious. These two in particular, with these bowing-down stalks and heavenly lights (verse 9) that match the number of other people in the family, seem obvious.

This suggests that Joseph knew his brothers would understand what he was saying, or he figured they were utterly stupid. Neither one was good.

I think it is also safe to assume that this moment didn't come out of nowhere. This was undoubtedly a pattern for this favored son to behave this way. After all, we are told that, after hearing about this first dream, his brothers "hated him *even more*" (verse 8; italics added; also verse 5). We are not told that his brothers started to hate him. They already hated him. The intensity of it was just ramping up, and Joseph kept throwing gasoline on the fire with his second dream.

Joseph was at least partly responsible for the broken relationships here. Surely, he detected the animosity. Perhaps he even enjoyed it. These familial connections were obviously broken and had been for a long time. Technically, these men were all brothers—technically.

But what does it mean to be a brother? Is it just to have at least one parent in common, or is there something more? Was Reuben's plea (verses 21-22) based on any shared bond, or was it solely driven by duty? For the others, the biological tie was not enough. But why?

What is required for you to call someone a brother or a sister?

Families Repeat Patterns

Jacob did something extraordinary in this passage: He scolded Joseph (Genesis 37:10). It is extraordinary because it was out of character. Up to this point, he had favored this son, giving him privileges above the others. Why was Joseph so favored?

The easy answer is that Joseph was the first one born to Jacob's favorite wife. Then the family drama was confined to this generation. However, in fact, we see that there is a long history of favored sons. Jacob was favored by his mother over Esau, and that resulted in his blessing. Jacob's father, Isaac, was favored over his brother, Ishmael. As a result, Ishmael was cast out to die in the wilderness.

Is it any wonder that Joseph's dreams and favor made the other brothers nervous? They undoubtedly knew the history, and they could see where this story was heading. Family patterns like this do carry down, oftentimes for generations. The more ingrained they get, the harder they are to dislodge. Some of us may not even recognize these patterns until we study our family history in some depth. Family history is not always as obvious as this one favored brother pattern is.

I examined my family history in seminary when I was assigned to work on my family's genogram. A genogram is similar to a family tree, except that once you have put together your tree, you go back and mark things such as addictions or troubled relationships or careers, for example. What then emerge are distinct patterns.

I had dreaded this assignment the whole of my seminary career, due in large part to the family's size, but also due to its complex history. What I learned about us, however, was invaluable. For instance, in my family, we noticed a tendency for young men to be reckless with money, but then the birth of their first child would bring that to a halt. We also noticed a tendency for our people to serve as soldiers, police officers, or pastors or to serve jail time.

Both of these tendencies are instructive as I raise a son in this family structure. It was fascinating, once I had it all mapped out, to see what showed up over and over. But it was also sad to see how regularly we passed down destructive behavior.

How do we break the cycle? It is not easy. First, we have to recognize that the patterns are there. Then we have to name what is unhealthy about those patterns. And then we have to choose, consciously and intentionally, to do something different. It is a struggle. It is almost as if those patterns are built into our DNA, but they are not. God gives us free will, which means that we have the capacity to choose another way of being. Actually doing that, however, is a much deeper struggle.

What patterns do you see showing up from generation to generation in your family?

Keeping It All in the (Broken) Family

And speaking of consequences to family patterns, did you catch who Joseph's brothers sold him to? Midianite traders. Or maybe Ishmaelites. Which one?

Possibly, these two names were used interchangeably, that the tribes were equivalents or they were so similar that, in the telling of this story, these people have been conflated. Some scholars have suggested that perhaps there were several oral traditions about this story of Joseph. In one of the stories, the traders were assumed to be Midianites; in the other, they were assumed to be Ishmaelites.

Maybe they were just so close to each other they might as well have been family. Actually, they were. Many of us probably recognize who the Ishmaelites were. These would be the descendants of Ishmael, Abraham's first son, the one born to Sarah's servant Hagar. In her anger or jealousy or because she was trying to protect her son, Isaac, Sarah demanded that Abraham cast out Hagar and Ishmael. God rescued them and promised that Ishmael would also have many descendants.

But Ishmael and Isaac weren't Abraham's only sons. After Sarah died, Abraham married Keturah, and Keturah gave birth to many sons, including one named Midian (Genesis 25:2). So it turns out that the Midianites were also sons of Abraham. Of course, we also know that Abraham's son with Sarah—Isaac—was the father of Jacob, and Jacob was the father of Joseph and his brothers. So whether the traders were Midianites or Ishmaelites, Joseph was sold to his cousins. And these would not have been terribly distant cousins. This was only three generations down from a shared father.

That shared father made decisions that complicated family. While often the finger points at Sarah for the division between Isaac and Ishmael, it was ultimately Abraham's decision.

Additionally, Abraham decided to remarry after Sarah's death and extend the family even more. His sons had all become separate tribes. They did not stay together. And it is possible, especially if the traders recognized these Israelites, that the resentment and sibling rivalry resulting from Abraham's favoring one son over the others carried down to that moment. So whichever traders they were, Ishmaelite or Midianite, they may have been happy to punish Israel.

And is it any wonder Joseph's brothers behaved this way? Relationships between brothers in this family had always been less than ideal. And fathers had not always helped things along well. Sure, Jacob did scold Joseph here. But did you also notice that he "took careful note of the matter" (37:11)? Jacob thought the dream could be true. If the other brothers detected their father's attitude, then the rivalry would only intensify. Disaster was on the horizon.

How are we shaped by the decisions others make?

More Than a Mistake

All of us who have siblings have probably had our "I could sell this person to traders" moments. My brother once announced that he was going to run away from home, and I helped him pack. Of course, as I watched out the window and saw him dragging his bag down the road, I ran to my mom and told her where he went so she could go get him.

Most all of us have had those thoughts, but few of us actually act on them. Few of us bring harm upon our brothers and sisters deliberately. Perhaps that is why Reuben felt safe enough to wander away from watching the cistern. Sure, the brothers had threatened murder, but it had been pretty easy to convince them to just throw Joseph in a well. Probably it was all talk, right?

Except it wasn't all talk. They went ahead with harm. No, they didn't murder him. They sold him. There was still no guarantee what would happen to him. He could have been beaten to death or forced into an army and killed in battle. They did not sell him into guaranteed safety. They sold him into who-knew-what, and they seem not to have cared one way or another about that.

These brothers went to extraordinary means to rid themselves of Joseph. To untangle the damage they had done would take extraordinary grace. It would take extraordinary grace working in the lives of Joseph and the people he would encounter as a slave. And it would take extraordinary grace working in the lives and hearts of these jealous and violent brothers.

Thankfully, as we will see as Joseph's story unfolds, God was up for the challenge. That is good news, for all of us. We may not sell our siblings into slavery, but we all do things we know aren't right in the course of our lifetime. Thankfully, God knows how to meet us in those situations and start working "all things together for good for the ones who love God" (Romans 8:28).

When have you needed God's extraordinary grace?

Lord, we are thankful that, when we get caught in destructive patterns, your grace is always creatively at work. Help us free ourselves from our broken past; in Jesus' name we pray. Amen.

The Spiritual Practice of Forgiveness

"Holding onto anger is like drinking poison and expecting the other person to die." Perhaps you have heard that expression. If anger is the poison, then forgiveness is the antidote. Anger and true forgiveness cannot coexist. One wipes out the other.

But forgiveness as a spiritual discipline? That implies forgiveness takes some work. Yes. Yes, it does. We sometimes have this mistaken perception that, over time, forgiveness just washes over us. Or we think that our offering forgiveness is contingent on someone wanting to be forgiven. If that person says the right thing or does something to make amends, then we can forgive that person.

Except that is not how it works at all. Well, I won't say "at all" because sometimes those things do contribute to our ability to forgive. Forgiveness, though, has more to do with the transformation of our own hearts. It should not be dependent on the work others do, but instead should be dependent on the work God does on us and what we are willing to receive from God.

Joseph's story is a profound narrative of the power of forgiveness. Joseph had every reason to be bitter and angry, but what if he had held on to that anger? How would his story have changed?

If Joseph had been surly, would he have been sold to Potiphar or marked to a much lower bidder? If he had been sulking and furious, would he have willingly offered to interpret the other two prisoners' dreams or even been offered the opportunity to attend to them? Would his resentment have kept him from sharing an interpretation generously with Pharaoh? And could his anger have kept him from saving his family, and the whole family of God, in the midst of a famine?

Instead, along the way, Joseph found ways to step into God's transformative love. We can do the same, but only if our hearts are open to it. But when they are, not only are we transformed, the people and circumstances around us are, too.

Focal Passage: Genesis 39:1-21
Background Text: Genesis 39:1–40:23
Purpose Statement: To recognize that God's grace doesn't eliminate all tough times

Genesis 39:1-21
¹**When Joseph had been taken down to Egypt, Potiphar, Pharaoh's chief officer, the commander of the royal guard and an Egyptian, purchased him from the Ishmaelites who had brought him down there. ²The LORD was with Joseph, and he became a successful man and served in his Egyptian master's household. ³His master saw that the LORD was with him and that the Lord made everything he did successful. ⁴Potiphar thought highly of Joseph, and Joseph became his assistant; he appointed Joseph head of his household and put everything he had under Joseph's supervision. ⁵From the time he appointed Joseph head of his household and of everything he had, the Lord blessed the Egyptian's household because of Joseph. The Lord blessed everything he had, both in the household and in the field. ⁶So he handed over everything he had to Joseph and didn't pay attention to anything except the food he ate.**

Now Joseph was well-built and handsome.

⁷**Some time later, his master's wife became attracted to Joseph and said, "Sleep with me."**

⁸He refused and said to his master's wife, "With me here, my master doesn't pay attention to anything in his household; he's put everything he has under my supervision. ⁹No one is greater than I am in this household, and he hasn't denied me anything except you, since you are his wife. How could I do this terrible thing and sin against God?" ¹⁰Every single day she tried to convince him, but he wouldn't agree to sleep with her or even to be with her.

¹¹One day when Joseph arrived at the house to do his work, none of the household's men were there. ¹²She grabbed his garment, saying, "Lie down with me." But he left his garment in her hands and ran outside. ¹³When she realized that he had left his garment in her hands and run outside, ¹⁴she summoned the men of her house and said to them, "Look, my husband brought us a Hebrew to ridicule us. He came to me to lie down with me, but I screamed. ¹⁵When he heard me raise my voice and scream, he left his garment with me and ran outside." ¹⁶She kept his garment with her until Joseph's master came home, ¹⁷and she told him the same thing: "The Hebrew slave whom you brought to us, to ridicule me, came to me; ¹⁸but when I raised my voice and screamed, he left his garment with me and ran outside."

¹⁹When Joseph's master heard the thing that his wife told him, "This is what your servant did to me," he was incensed. ²⁰Joseph's master took him and threw him in jail, the place where the king's prisoners were held. While he was in jail, ²¹the Lord was with Joseph and remained loyal to him. He caused the jail's commander to think highly of Joseph.

Key Verses: "Joseph's master took him and threw him in jail, the place where the king's prisoners were held. While he was in jail, the LORD was with Joseph and remained loyal to him. He caused the jail's commander to think highly of Joseph" (Genesis 39:20-21).

I was a senior in high school, standing in a circle of seven girls in our journalism class. We were debating whether to do an article on violence in teenage relationships for our school newspaper, as it was a topic that had recently become prevalent in the news. We wondered if it was applicable to anyone. That was the question we had to ask. It turns out, we had the answer.

We went around the circle as each girl disclosed her own story of attack and abuse. Of the seven of us, five had a story to tell. Two of us just looked shocked at what they were hearing—except I knew otherwise. I knew one of the ones who acted shocked had been attacked by her boyfriend. I knew because I'd hidden her from him for a couple of days while she healed enough to show her face again.

So six of the seven of us had been attacked. We had the answer to our question of whether it was applicable. And so . . . we didn't do the story. What was the point? Who would believe us anyway?

Another interesting detail about this story is that five of the seven of us were church-going young women, and six of the seven of us would have confessed faith in Christ. Nonetheless, we faced threat and danger. So did Joseph. Following God was not protecting us from life. So what was it doing for us? Where is the power in our faith when we find ourselves in powerless moments? Joseph's encounter with Potiphar's wife helps us unpack this question.

Power and Privilege

Each summer, United Methodist Women offers a phenomenal opportunity for study and growth in discipleship at Mission u (*unitedmethodistwomen.org/mission-u*). In 2019, I had the opportunity to teach the Practicing Resurrection study, based on the Gospel of Mark. One of the exercises we were invited to do was to name our own social location. We did this by listing things such as where we live, our gender, our race/ethnicity, our economic status, our educational level, and so forth.

Once we listed these, we were then invited to place a star beside the ones that were privileged states. I scanned my list. I had only one that was not starred. Otherwise, I was loaded down with privilege and power.

I was honestly shocked. I fully expected to be unprivileged in at least half of the categories. But there I sat, staring my privilege in the face. Then I wondered why I was so surprised. If I think back on my life, of course, I have had struggles and have been through traumatic events. In the midst of those, however, I always had food to eat and a roof over my head. My safety net is wide and sturdy. That is a sign of privilege.

We humans have a tendency to focus on our negative experiences, though. I think the reason I thought I lacked power and privilege is because the situations where I have felt powerless seem so vivid. In reality, they are vivid because they are exceptional. But because they seem so significant in my mind, they feel more prevalent in my life than they actually are.

Which has me now thinking about Potiphar's wife. She was also incredibly privileged, and perhaps she was primarily behaving in such a way, expecting that what she wanted from Joseph she could have (Genesis 39:7). However, I wonder if she was also coming from a position of being focused on her powerlessness as well.

We are told in the passage that Joseph was given authority over everything in Potiphar's house (verses 4-5) because Potiphar "didn't pay any attention to anything except the food he ate" (verse 6). Did that include his wife? We do learn later that Potiphar had restricted access to her, but we do not know that he paid attention to her.

So was Potiphar's wife seeking attention from Joseph because she did not get attention from Potiphar? Did she feel as trapped and powerless as Joseph did? If so, did that motivate her treatment of Joseph as well? In other words, was she taking what power she had in a powerless situation and using it? This does not justify her behavior. However, it may help us see how broken the entire situation was from the beginning.

When have you felt powerless, and when have you had power that you did not recognize you had?

Who Gets Heard?

Potiphar's wife was being ignored. Her husband was not paying much attention to her, obviously. The text only partially tells her story. We do not know much about her other than that she was married to Potiphar but attracted to Joseph. We don't even know her name.

She was totally defined by the men she was related to or the men she was trying to relate to. No one was listening to her story—well, except when she told Joseph's story, or at least her version of Joseph's story.

Joseph had his own story, too. He was attacked by a woman who demanded that he sleep with her (Genesis 39:7, 12). That is a story of sexual harassment and abuse. When she could not get her way, she had Joseph punished, turning the story against him (verses 13-19). He was not in a position to defend himself or to demand of her. He did not have the power. He was the victim. When his story could not be told, he was victimized again.

It is an important part of healing for victims to get to tell their stories when they are ready. But it is also critical in that moment that their story is believed. Joseph had no way to prove his story, so in the absence of proof, power always wins. No one believes the powerless, even though the powerless virtually cannot engage in such abuse.

That is why the #metoo movement of a few years ago was such a watershed. This movement against sexual abuse and sexual harassment gave individuals a forum in which they could tell of their experiences at the hands of the powerful and the privileged. It gave credence to the stories, if simply because of the sheer number.

The deluge reminded me of that moment in high school. I thought then that the reported statistics on sexual abuse were low, and #metoo confirmed it. And then #churchtoo just added to the devastation. This movement seeks to bring into awareness the sexual harassment, abuse, and assault that happens within churches and faith communities.

Joseph's story, and #churchtoo especially, prove that faith in God does not guarantee our safety. There are accidents. There are mistakes. And there are powerful and sin-twisted people who seek their pleasure, even at the cost of others' harm. The victims and victimizers desperately need to know God's presence in their lives. But in moments like that, where is God?

How do you create space to hear stories that people tell that are painful for them to share?

Where Is God?

The text for this lesson is interesting because it opens by telling us that the Lord was with Joseph, and it closes the same way (Genesis 39:2, 23). However, those two conditions were vastly different. First, the Lord was with Joseph in lifting him out of slavery to put him as an overseer in a prominent man's house. Then, the Lord was with Joseph while he was in jail. Up and down, beginning and end, God was there.

But what about in the middle? Where was God when Joseph was trying to navigate the challenge of Potiphar's wife? Why is the text silent about God's presence then?

The day-to-day. That is what is taking place in the middle of this passage. Joseph was managing the household. He was also facing a significant challenge. That challenge would ultimately cause him to lose his position and end up in jail. It is then that the text notes that God was back on the scene. However, we are just told that God was "with" Joseph.

Joseph's interaction with God was different than his ancestors' interactions with God. God showed up and wrestled with his father, chatted with his grandmother, and walked with his great-grandfather. God was just "with" Joseph. But how?

So is God with us in the day-to-day? This passage feels like life feels so often. It is easy to get caught up in our routines. It is easy to get focused on the work that is before us. It is easy to miss the presence of God in those moments that we have all the time.

Why is it that we tend to recognize God's presence in emergencies? Maybe it is because that is when we need God's presence. When relying on our own ability fails, or when we find ourselves in situations too difficult for us to manage alone, then we turn and look for God. Then we see God at work in our lives.

Isn't it true, though, that God was always with Joseph? Joseph's faith and ethics probably made him a good and trusted manager and helped him respond with integrity to Potiphar's wife. Faith formation is a mark of God's presence in our lives. Just because the text does not mention God specifically through these events does not mean God was not present.

It may also be the case that the author of this story assumes that we know God is with us when things are going well. It is more important, then, to name that God is also with us in the difficult times. When it comes to sharing our faith, we need to name that God is with us through all things: the good, the bad, and the ugly, too.

How do you experience God's presence in the everyday?

Grace in All Things

We affirm that God's grace is present throughout our journey of faith. We may have dramatic moments of encountering such grace, such as if we have a moment of conversion like a lightning bolt moment or a moment when, like John Wesley, our hearts are "strangely warmed."

Wesley talked about God's grace as a lifelong journey with God. God goes ahead of us in prevenient grace. God is with us in justifying grace when we recognize God's salvific power over our sin to redeem us. We experience God's transformative presence as we grow in faith in sanctifying grace.

Joseph's story illustrates that journey for us beautifully, but also shows how there are moments when the faith journey seems less linear than that description might imply. There are stops and starts. God's will seems to be at work, sometimes thwarted and then adjusted as the story unfolds. But all along the way, in quiet and dramatic ways, God continues to show up.

Joseph's journey is our journey, too. We may not have as dramatic a rise as to ultimately become second-in-command of Egypt, but we have our moments when God is particularly at work loving and blessing us in ways that are meaningful for us. Sometimes it is hard to see those moments in the pressure of the reality of them. And certainly during hard times, it can be difficult to see God, but God's grace persists.

You may feel unheard, you may be unjustly persecuted, you may struggle to do the right thing when the right thing will undoubtedly lead to loss. You may face abuse or harassment, which is outside the will of God for your life. But God will still be there, fighting for you, and doing all God can to work in all things for good. We will see, as Joseph's story continues to unfold, how profound that work can be.

When have you experienced God's loving presence of grace in surprising times?

Lord, we are grateful that you are the kind of God who keeps showing up in all our struggles and triumphs; in Jesus' name we pray. Amen.

Focal Passage: Genesis 41:1-16, 25-32
Background Text: Genesis 41:1-57
Purpose Statement: To realize the expanse of God's grace

Genesis 41:1-16, 25-32

¹Two years later, Pharaoh dreamed that he was standing near the Nile. ²In front of him, seven healthy-looking, fattened cows climbed up out of the Nile and grazed on the reeds. ³Just then, seven other cows, terrible-looking and scrawny, climbed up out of the Nile after them and stood beside them on the bank of the Nile. ⁴The terrible-looking, scrawny cows devoured the seven healthy-looking, fattened cows. Then Pharaoh woke up. ⁵He went back to sleep and had a second dream, in which seven ears of grain, full and healthy, grew on a single stalk. ⁶Just then, seven ears of grain, scrawny and scorched by the east wind, sprouted after them, ⁷and the scrawny ears swallowed up the full and well-formed ears. Then Pharaoh woke up and realized it was a dream. ⁸In the morning, he was disturbed and summoned all of Egypt's religious experts and all of its advisors. Pharaoh described his dreams to them, but they couldn't interpret them for Pharaoh.

⁹Then the chief wine steward spoke to Pharaoh: "Today I've just remembered my mistake. ¹⁰Pharaoh was angry with his servants and put me and the chief baker under arrest with the commander of the royal guard. ¹¹We both dreamed one night, he and I, and each of our dreams had its own interpretation.

[12]A young Hebrew man, a servant of the commander of the royal guard, was with us. We described our dreams to him, and he interpreted our dreams for us, giving us an interpretation for each dream. [13]His interpretations came true exactly: Pharaoh restored me to my position but hanged him."

[14]So Pharaoh summoned Joseph, and they quickly brought him from the dungeon. He shaved, changed clothes, and appeared before Pharaoh. [15]Pharaoh said to Joseph, "I had a dream, but no one could interpret it. Then I heard that when you hear a dream, you can interpret it."

[16]Joseph answered Pharaoh, "It's not me. God will give Pharaoh a favorable response." . . .

[25]Joseph said to Pharaoh, "Pharaoh has actually had one dream. God has announced to Pharaoh what he is about to do. [26]The seven healthy cows are seven years, and the seven healthy ears of grain are seven years. It's actually one dream. [27]The seven thin and frail cows, climbing up after them, are seven years. The seven thin ears of grain, scorched by the east wind, are seven years of famine. [28]It's just as I told Pharaoh: God has shown Pharaoh what he is about to do. [29]Seven years of great abundance are now coming throughout the entire land of Egypt. [30]After them, seven years of famine will appear, and all of the abundance in the land of Egypt will be forgotten. The famine will devastate the land. [31]No one will remember the abundance in the land because the famine that follows will be so very severe.

32The dream occurred to Pharaoh twice because God has determined to do it, and God will make it happen soon.

Key Verse: "Joseph answered Pharaoh, 'It's not me. God will give Pharaoh a favorable response'" (Genesis 41:16).

"Is anyone else dreaming the most vivid dreams of your life right now?" A friend posed the question on Facebook during the midst of the COVID-19 quarantine, and everyone's imaginations were working overtime. My dreams were vivid but not the most vivid of my life.

I've been gifted (or plagued) with an entertaining sleeping brain. When I was a young child, I experienced night terrors of a dinosaur stealing my tricycle and had the recurring dream where I pricked my finger on the spinning wheel like Sleeping Beauty. As an adult, I've had dreams that helped me work out the path God has for me.

The year I was discerning a call to ministry, I had a whole series of dreams in which I would be going about my business, and then something surprising would happen. I would feel the breath get knocked out of me, and I would pass out. Then I would wake up in the dream, calm and rested, in the church. I also had a dream where I was going about my average tasks, like cleaning and working and visiting with people, all while wearing a cardinal's miter.

Were these dreams my subconscious mind working out the pull from God on my life to go into the ministry, or were the dreams visions given to me by God? I don't know. It doesn't matter to me. Either way, they led to the same results: God had a purpose for my life.

God had a purpose for Joseph, too. How many obstacles would Joseph have to confront, though? How many people would have to see and experience the workings of God for everything to come together, and how would everyone get the message?

These Dreams

We have scientific explanations for dreams these days. Well, sort of. Dreams remain, on some level, a mystery. Everyone from psychotherapists such as Sigmund Freud and Carl Jung to current neurobiologists have conjectured on the role and purpose of dreams.

Are they the workings of our subconscious mind revealing our deep desires and anxieties? Are they just random firings of neurons pulling different images from our memories together? Or are they practice scenarios our mind concocts to help us manage and prepare for potential threats? The answer is, we don't know.

In the ancient world, people understood dreams to be the way that humans encountered the realm of the gods. The ancients believed that dreams allowed them to see what the gods were doing without having to die to do so. For this reason, they often understood dreams to have prophetic purpose. If you entered the realm of the gods, it would make sense that the gods had a message for you, or at the very least you had seen something that might be helpful for other people to know.

We probably read this account from Joseph's life in Genesis 41 assuming that Joseph was gifted at interpreting dreams. We are reading, however, knowing the end of the story. Up to this point, Joseph had dreams that he shared with his family, but he did not actually interpret those dreams (though clearly his father and brothers did). Those dreams had not come true—yet. In fact, at this point, those dreams looked way off-base.

Joseph had, in Genesis 40, correctly interpreted the dreams of the wine steward and the baker. Actually, it is more accurate to say that, according to Joseph, God gave him the correct interpretation. So at this point in the story, it looks as though Joseph had been right about one set of dreams but had missed on the other. What would happen next?

Joseph being brought before Pharaoh would be a great test of the partnership between God and Joseph in interpreting dreams. There were life-and-death consequences. If Joseph lied to Pharaoh, he undoubtedly would face the same fate as the baker. But the interpretation of the dream had the potential to save lives, too. If Pharaoh listened and a famine came, people would not starve to death. What would unfold: salvation or destruction?

Do you dream? If so, how have your dreams prepared you for something that was on the horizon?

Working All Things Together for Good?

Before Joseph even heard Pharaoh's description of his dreams, he again credited God with the interpretation of them (Genesis 41:16). In the previous lesson, we noted that God did not show up and talk with Joseph as God had done for his ancestors. God was a presence here, though, in this wisdom. It seems, too, that God had a plan not only for Joseph in this moment, but God had a plan for Pharaoh and for all of Egypt as well.

But what was that plan? Well, since we have been told over and over that God was with Joseph, and because we know the end of the story, we figure the plan was to save the world through Joseph and Pharaoh. God had walked along with Joseph through ups and downs and was working every awful event when people chose to behave in evil and destructive ways to work things around to where blessing occurred instead.

Yes, that interpretation is a comfortable one for me, because it affirms that God does not inflict pain and suffering. Instead, God works to rescue and redeem us from the pain we inflict on one another or the suffering that occurs simply because we live in a broken world, one that includes drought and famine because the natural world is out of order. That interpretation does, however, ignore a detail in the text.

When Joseph was concluding the dream interpretation, he mentioned, "The dream occurred to Pharaoh twice because God has determined to do it, and God will make it happen soon" (Genesis 41:32). Wait. Does that mean God had decided to bring drought and famine on the world? Even if Egypt was prepared, the rest of the known world would suffer. Only those who had the means to bargain with Egypt would stand a chance of making it through these times. How can our good and loving God deliberately create conditions of suffering and death?

When have you been tempted to credit God for difficulties in your life?

All-Inclusive God

In this case, it is important to place this story of Joseph in the larger biblical narrative. This story is the bridge between the establishment of the Abrahamic family as the covenant people of God that we read in Genesis and the story of their liberation from Egypt in Exodus. Joseph's story explains how that move was made, but it may also be that Joseph's story was a story of missed opportunity for Pharaoh.

In explaining that these dreams were interpreted by God and that the drought and famine were determined by God (Genesis 41:25-32), yet God's grace and provision extended to Pharaoh and all of Egypt, Joseph was sharing with Pharaoh where the real power over all creation lies. As more of this truth unfolded, as things happened exactly as Joseph explained, Pharaoh could have recognized who the true God is.

Instead, Pharaoh recognized Joseph as gifted. He placed his faith in the power of a man who apparently had access to a god. Pharaoh also maintained his control over Joseph. Joseph was second in charge. Pharaoh maintained his supremacy. He kept his power, but missed the point.

Nonetheless, God worked through the centralized and well-resourced Egyptian government to save not only Egypt, but essentially the known world. God worked through those who did not explicitly believe in order to do salvific work.

Perhaps, then, it was not so much that God ordained the drought, but that God knew the drought was coming and was determined to work within the best organized system to keep as many people alive as possible. Additionally, with Joseph in place, God provided for the ones who believed as well.

I am still in awe that God came after me. Those dreams that came to me came only two years after I was baptized. They also came when I was struggling to recover from the trauma of a school shooting. I was not in a place to see the future God had for me. But there were those dreams, as well as other quiet and not-so-quiet moments, when God seemed to be drawing me into a life of ministry. God was making it too obvious to miss. Looking back, I was stunned at how many pieces seemed to get moved into place to call me to God. What a wonder-working, creative Creator!

There are no limits to God's grace. God's love and provision cover the whole world, whether that world recognizes this or not. Our God is all-inclusive.

When have you seen God's presence active in the life of someone who does not believe in God?

Foundations in Our Faith

This moment in Joseph's story shows us how pervasive God's provision is. We affirm that God is seeking to be in relationship with everyone. God is infinitely creative in how God gets our attention.

We see that creativity in working all throughout the broken reality of Joseph's story. Jealous brothers sold him into slavery, but he rose in prominence in Potiphar's house. Potiphar's wife acted out of desperate desire to have attention, and that landed Joseph in jail. But God helped Joseph interpret the dreams of two prominent prisoners. Years later, that worked out for Joseph, who then became second-in-command of all Egypt (Genesis 41:40). If that is not proof of God's creativity and prevalence, I don't know what is.

That is prevenient grace at its best, the grace that goes before. We stumble blindly through life sometimes, not seeing the miraculous way God is clearing our paths. But when we do look around and see what a stunning path

God has cleared for us, often in the midst of our own misguided wanderings or in situations where people have actively intended us harm, we can't help but be amazed.

A God who pays attention to an overly spoiled son who tries to reach a self-centered pharaoh and who works to save the covenant family who is not behaving like a covenant family should—that is a God we do not deserve. But that is the God we get any way!

The pharaohs of Egypt enslaved people to build structures that have literally stood the test of time, but the faith of the Egyptians has long since faded. The foundations of our faith were built on those same sands, but they were founded on a God who loves so fully and eternally, that foundation will never shift, no matter how much the sand moves.

What an amazing grace! May we never be blind to it! May we always see!

When has God's grace overwhelmed you?

Lord, we don't deserve you, but we are grateful for you; in Jesus' name we pray. Amen.

Focal Passage: Genesis 45:1-15
Background Text: Genesis 42:1–45:27
Purpose Statement: To understand that we receive grace in order to give grace.

Genesis 45:1-15

[1]Joseph could no longer control himself in front of all his attendants, so he declared, "Everyone, leave now!" So no one stayed with him when he revealed his identity to his brothers. [2]He wept so loudly that the Egyptians and Pharaoh's household heard him. [3]Joseph said to his brothers, "I'm Joseph! Is my father really still alive?" His brothers couldn't respond because they were terrified before him.

[4]Joseph said to his brothers, "Come closer to me," and they moved closer. He said, "I'm your brother Joseph! The one you sold to Egypt. [5]Now, don't be upset and don't be angry with yourselves that you sold me here. Actually, God sent me before you to save lives. [6]We've already had two years of famine in the land, and there are five years left without planting or harvesting. [7]God sent me before you to make sure you'd survive and to rescue your lives in this amazing way. [8]You didn't send me here; it was God who made me a father to Pharaoh, master of his entire household, and ruler of the whole land of Egypt.

[9]"Hurry! Go back to your father. Tell him this is what your son Joseph says: 'God has made me master of all

of Egypt. Come down to me. Don't delay. [10]You may live in the land of Goshen, so you will be near me, your children, your grandchildren, your flocks, your herds, and everyone with you. [11]I will support you there, so you, your household, and everyone with you won't starve, since the famine will still last five years.' [12]You and my brother Benjamin have seen with your own eyes that I'm speaking to you. [13]Tell my father about my power in Egypt and about everything you've seen. Hurry and bring my father down here." [14]He threw his arms around his brother Benjamin's neck and wept, and Benjamin wept on his shoulder. [15]He kissed all of his brothers and wept, embracing them. After that, his brothers were finally able to talk to him.

Key Verse: "Now, don't be upset and don't be angry with yourselves that you sold me here. Actually, God sent me before you to save lives" (Genesis 45:5).

DISCIPLE Bible Study. I have participated in it four times, once as a participant and three times as a leader. Every single time, I have seen lives transformed by it. People don't expect to be so moved by a somewhat intense, year-long study of the Scriptures; but then we too often discount the transformative power of engaging the Word.

In one of the groups I was leading, a woman came to a revelation. She realized that she had been carrying around anger from a situation in which she was attacked. She had such rage for the person who attacked her, and it was eating her alive. She had never been able to move past that moment. But the deeper she delved into Scripture, the more people she encountered who forgave those who had wronged them.

Joseph's was one of those stories for her. Jesus hanging on the cross and asking God to forgive those who had nailed him to it was another. So one night, she said, "I am going to forgive him. I am going to forgive the person who attacked me. I am going to let go of the anger. I am going to do it so I can live freely in the love of God again."

It was a powerful release to witness. It was as though we saw a young woman transform into a new being before our eyes. It was one more thing that convinced us all that there is life after death.

Sometimes letting go of past wounds is exactly what we need to do to have a bountiful future. How do we let go of those wounds though? Through forgiveness, sure, but we are empowered to offer that kind of forgiveness because we have the grace of God in our lives.

Forgive . . . and Forget?

It was one of those conversations over a cup of coffee and two hearts. The older woman was sharing bits of her life story with the younger one. They were sharing the deep heartaches of their lives, those betrayals that feel like the end of the world. Except they aren't the end of the world, are they? Both of these women had persevered.

Still, there were hard things. The older woman looked deep into the younger woman's eyes and said, "You know, along this path of my life, I have had to choose. I can't choose what other people do to me. I can't choose how other people feel about me. But I can choose how I feel. I can choose what I do. And I have chosen to forgive. I have chosen to let go of the resentment and the anger. And I have chosen joy instead."

But did she choose to forget? No. Forgetting would have meant letting go of the lessons. Forgetting would have meant opening herself up to more pain. Forgetting would have meant abandoning her story.

We can remember what we have been through without being captive to the anger and the pain. In fact, that may be a powerful way to heal from past hurts. Jim Rendon's work *Upside: The New Science of Post-Traumatic Growth* explores just such a view. He points out that our stories give us meaning, particularly when we can take those stories and respond in helpful ways to others.

Joseph did exactly that. He chose to forgive, but he did not forget. He could name what his brothers had done. But what he did was to turn his story into something with meaning. He chose not to focus on the hurt and the harm, but instead to see what good his story had created (Genesis 45:5-8). It did not excuse the actions of his brothers. It did, however, redeem those actions. God took what was meant for evil in Joseph's life and turned it into good. If there was ever a powerful proof of God's work, this is it.

But the story remains. It is not forgotten. We are still telling that story millennia later. We are still learning from that story, too. Whenever you face a journey of healing, don't ever let someone tell you that you have to let go of the story. Find meaning in it instead.

When have you found good in something tragic that has happened in your life?

God's Providence

Theologians debate what we mean when we talk about God's providence. One way of understanding God's providence is that God foresees all things and works all things to the divine will. We could certainly understand the story of Joseph in those terms. But was God manipulating all the action, or was God working within the actions of people to bring things that might have been directed toward evil to good? Again, we could understand Joseph's story both ways. Joseph certainly laid all the credit on God and, consequently, none of the blame on his brothers. As Joseph told the story, everything that happened had been God's design.

Still, would God sell someone into slavery? put him in a difficult situation with a boss's wife? leave him in prison for years? That certainly doesn't seem like a good and loving God.

If we understand divine providence in terms of God controlling all actions, though, then that must be what we understand God to have done. This understanding also means that no one in the story acted with free will, that the brothers didn't choose to sell Joseph into slavery, and that Joseph didn't choose to forgive them. It was all the work of God. In this way of understanding, no one had a choice in the matter at all.

There is another way of understanding God's providence, a way proposed by Methodist theologian Charles Wood. Holding to the understanding that a loving God gives all of us free will to choose, even as God coaxes us to try to follow the way of life God has for us, God will nonetheless allow us to make horrible decisions.

However, within that reality, God provides. In particular, God provides God. With this understanding, God did not manipulate Joseph's story. Instead, God provided within the decisions and the actions that people took, and that provision brought life.

God provided an interpretation of dreams to a willing Joseph, and that saved Egypt. It was in the process of saving the known world. It would consequently also save the covenant family of God, but God was not done providing.

Joseph's family would settle in Goshen, located on the Nile delta (Genesis 45:10-11).

The Nile was absolutely predictable. You could set your clocks (if they had clocks) by the Nile floods. It also meant that the delta was predictably rich farmland. That Joseph's family would be able to settle in such a space was a great gift. It was an incredible work of God's provision, and it was an unbelievable gift of grace.

How would you define or describe God's providence?

Grace Upon Grace Upon Grace

Grace is the loving presence of God in our lives. Sometimes that presence is palpable and obvious. Other times, though, it is far quieter. In an earlier lesson, we noted that God was not an active character in the Joseph story. God is mentioned over and over and over, but God never actually "showed up" for Joseph as God did for some of his ancestors.

It seems more like God was felt. But was God felt in the moments when it happened? In other words, was Joseph confident that God was with him in prison, or was it only after he had been elevated to the top man in Pharaoh's household that he saw God?

We have confidence that Joseph remained a person of faith throughout the story, such as when he credited God with interpreting the dreams. But did Joseph feel God working in his life in those times? We can't know, because we only have the story that is in front of us. The story in front of us narrates God's presence throughout Joseph's life, but this narrative was also written after everything happened. Hindsight could indeed be 20/20.

But sometimes that is how grace works for us, too. Sometimes it is difficult to see all the ways grace is working in our lives. It is not until we look back and notice all the road markers that we see how often and in what ways God was fighting for us. Our view is limited. If only we could look, as the song from *The Prince of Egypt* invites us to do, at our lives through heaven's eyes. My guess is, if we could, we would see miracle after miracle after miracle before us. We would see God's grace going before us, alongside us, and behind us throughout our lives.

Probably the most dramatic example of that hindsight for me came as a result of my call to ministry. It followed the pattern of prevenient, justifying, and sanctifying grace. But looking at this journey in reverse shows how hindsight revealed the pieces. I am now fully living that call as an ordained elder, still learning and growing into the pastor God is calling me to be but committed to journeying with the Holy Spirit for the whole of this life of sanctification.

My actual call was a lightning bolt moment that occurred when God showed up and answered the question I had for God. (Spoiler alert: That question is covered in the last lesson in this quarter.) That moment of conversion to the ministry, so to speak, was the point of justification for my call. But as I have looked back now aware of this call, I remember that I had taken an occupational fitness test in eighth grade that told me my highest aptitude for professions was minister or teacher. I thought that was weird since I didn't even go to church.

Then I majored in English, which focuses on the close analysis of a text to draw out greater meaning. I majored in that field without any intention of teaching, but I didn't know what I would do with it. I just knew it was what I was supposed to do.

And then I was the child/young adult who found herself walking alongside family members in the hospital and breaking news to them that someone died, which started when I was ten! There were many more pieces of the puzzle that, once I looked back, made my call fall into place. God had been present and working in those moments, even if I didn't recognize it at the time, just as God does when God is wooing us through prevenient grace.

Joseph saw God at work in his life through the thick and the thin, or at least he did in momentary bursts and with the benefit of perspective. Now that he had this perspective, though, it was not his to hold on to. It was his to share.

When have you looked back over your life and seen God at work in surprising ways?

Set Free to Live and to Love

Joseph received abundant grace. He could have hoarded up that grace greedily and considered it his special privilege of following God. But then, would he have received grace? Grace transforms us into people who love like Christ. Jesus was not greedy with love. Neither should we be.

Joseph's love extended to two significant groups in this story. First, it extended to the Egyptians. The Egyptians did not worship Joseph's God. We don't get an indication that they ever do; and in Moses' story, that division came to a violent head. But Joseph had received abundant life. Joseph would extend abundant life. There would be no restrictions. God shares without restriction, calls all of us to God. Joseph modeled the same.

Then Joseph extended love to his family, not just any family, but the brothers who meant to kill him and ultimately sold him into slavery. These were brothers who disregarded him out of anger and jealousy and, as far as

Joseph knew, had no regrets about that decision. Yes, they would be glad to see that Joseph was alive, but they were also fearful that he may do to them as they did to him. But Joseph had been transformed by God's love. Joseph would extend that love back to them.

The woman in the DISCIPLE Bible Study group mentioned before also had an opportunity to let go of anger and let God's love flow through her. Now, in her case, the loving thing to do for herself and her abuser was not to have contact with that abuser. She knew not to risk that abuse might occur again. But when she accepted God's transformative peace through forgiveness and grace, she was set free of old ways of being that held her captive. Then she was free to love others more abundantly.

That is how God's grace can work for all of us. As we grow toward perfection in love, we can let go of fears and anger and hate and malice. We can be set free of all burdens to fully live and deeply love. What a miracle!

What moments from your past need to be transformed by God's grace so that you can fully live and love?

Lord of all time and all places, help us to love without restrictions so that we can help your grace transform the world; in Jesus' name we pray. Amen.

Daily Bible Readings (Unit 2)

June 28
Psalm 118:19-29

June 29
Exodus 20:13-17

June 30
Exodus 22:5-15

July 1
Proverbs 3:27-30

July 2
Proverbs 6:1-5

July 3
Proverbs 14:20-22

July 4
Proverbs 25:20-23

July 5
Hebrews 6:9-12

July 6
Deuteronomy
24:17-22

July 7
Job 29:11-17

July 8
Titus 1:5-9

July 9
Leviticus 19:18;
Matthew 19:16-22

July 10
Ruth 2:3-9

July 11
Ruth 2:10-16

July 12
Psalm 94:1-11

July 13
Isaiah 1:10-18

July 14
Acts 2:36-42

July 15
Acts 9:26-31

July 16
Luke 10:1-12

July 17
James 1:21-27

July 18
Acts 6:1-7

July 19
Acts 5:27-32,
40-42

July 20
Luke 7:36-50

July 21
Romans 2:1-8

July 22
2 Thessalonians
3:10-15

July 23
2 Corinthians
1:16-22

July 24
Matthew 13:53-58

July 25
Mark 2:1-12

Unit 2
The People Next Door

Oddly enough, everywhere I lived growing up, we had neighbors who were Jehovah's Witnesses. There were great advantages to that actually, chiefly being that our neighborhood was assumed to be covered, so we never had Jehovah's Witnesses knocking on our doors—well, except to see if we could come outside and play.

However, because their faith so dramatically shaped their lives, we also had ample opportunity to ask questions, to learn about their faith. It particularly came up when Christmas rolled around and our friends didn't get presents. While I did not agree with their interpretation of Scripture, I have come to appreciate how we lived life together and shared faith together, like neighbors should do.

We have, by and large, forgotten how to get to know our neighbors. There was a big push, as globalization has increased, to see our neighbors as the people who live on the other side of the world. That was a valuable challenge to our ethnocentricity, but it also distanced our interaction with our neighbors. We could send money to the other side of the world to help our neighbors; but somehow, at the same time, we eliminated our porches and moved indoors to focus on electronics, and we forgot how to live life with the people right next door.

We may be in a moment of correcting that reality. While I certainly hope the summer of 2021 is different, I write these words in the spring of 2020, when we are all confined to our houses. If there has been one blessing in this pandemic moment, though, it has been to remind us that there are people right next door to us. We have room enough in our hearts for neighbors near and far.

As the lessons in this unit unfold, we will see both of those populations as our neighbors. Let's live into both realities as the people called to love God and neighbor.

Focal Passage: Proverbs 3:27-30; 6:1-5; 25:20-23
Background Texts: Proverbs 3:27-30; 6:1-5; 14:20-22; 25:20-23
Purpose Statement: To acknowledge the risk in loving our neighbor

Proverbs 3:27-30

27Don't withhold good from someone who deserves it,
 when it is in your power to do so.
28Don't say to your neighbor, "Go and come back;
 I'll give it to you tomorrow," when you have it.
29Don't plan to harm your neighbor
 who trusts and lives near you.
30Don't accuse anyone without reason,
 when they haven't harmed you.

Proverbs 6:1-5

1My son, if you guarantee a loan for your neighbor
 or shake hands in agreement with a stranger,
2 you will be trapped by your words;
 you will be caught by your words.
3Do this, my son, to get out of it,
 for you have come under the control of your neighbor.
 So go, humble yourself, and pester your neighbor.
4Don't give sleep to your eyes
 or slumber to your eyelids.
5Get yourself free like a gazelle from a hunter,
 like a bird from the hand of a fowler.

Proverbs 25:20-23

²⁰Singing a song to a troubled heart
   is like taking off a garment on a cold day
   or putting vinegar on a wound.
²¹If your enemies are starving, feed them some bread;
   if they are thirsty, give them water to drink.
²²By doing this, you will heap burning coals on their heads,
   and the Lord will reward you.
²³The north wind stirs up rain,
   and a person who plots quietly provokes angry faces.

Key Verse: "Don't say to your neighbor, 'Go and come back; I'll give it to you tomorrow,' when you have it" (Proverbs 3:28).

The first house my parents owned was small by many American standards: 1,000 square feet, two bedrooms, one bathroom. The lot was a corner one, though, giving us more open land than the house itself actually occupied.

But Dad had noticed something odd about that land when he examined the deed. A one-foot strip on the south side actually appeared to belong to our neighbors, despite the fact that it was contained within our fence. To make certain, Dad had an assessor come out and mark the land. He included our neighbor in the discussion as the assessor confirmed what my dad had noticed. The assessor then explained something about squatting laws, that arguably the land would automatically deed over to us unless the neighbor maintained it.

My dad did not believe that was right and offered to pay the neighbor a fair price for the land. The neighbor, on the other hand, confirmed that he still had rights to that land. Yes, for a time, the assessor asserted. So the neighbor informed my father that, from then on, he would be mowing that strip of land. He would take no money for it, but neither would he let it go to us. He also would bring charges against us if we tried to maintain that land.

Since my father's mowing schedule never seemed to line up with the neighbor's, from then on, we always had one strip of land that was shorter or taller than the rest of the yard. And our relationship with the once kindly neighbor gradually soured as he more regularly accused us of trying to steal from him every time we played in that part of the yard.

When we move, we don't always know who will end up living next door. Even if we meet the people who currently live there, we cannot guarantee they will stay. And, like what happened with my family's neighbor, we can't assume that a relationship that starts out friendly will stay that way.

People are unpredictable. Living around others has risk. Nonetheless, as the people called to love God and neighbor, we are invited by Christ to take such risks. That is fine in theory, but what does it mean for us in real life?

Bad Fences Make Good Neighbors

Fences seem to be problems in my history with neighbors. But then, what are fences meant to do but keep us separated from one another? They create the "That's mine; this is yours" mentality.

That very mentality is what plagued our neighbor. For some reason, he could not stand that we had laid claim to something that was his by fencing it in, even though we did not actually install that fence but bought the property with the fence already in place. In our case, the old adage "Good fences make good neighbors" was not actually true. It was more accurate to say, "Good fences make bad neighbors."

That fence between us and those neighbors was a chain-link fence. In that case, it exacerbated our relationship because the neighbor could see every time my brother and I approached his strip of land, and he was quick to yell at us to stay back if he saw us. If we had a privacy fence, we might have played in peace. But privacy fences do not necessarily guarantee such neighborly distance in one another's lives, particularly when the fences fall down.

My husband, son, and I lived in a house in Texas where just such a fence fell down, a result of a strong windstorm and flooding. We didn't particularly need the fence, but our neighbor, who had a dog, did. That brought the man to our door for the first time after three years of living next to each other and only interacting on Halloween up to that point.

He came to ask us what we were doing about the fence. He brought proof that, technically, the fence was on our property. However, he had a request. Could he please have some say in the fence since we shared it? None of our three fence sides matched. We didn't care about the fence, but he was willing to work with us. If he could pick the fence, he would pay for half of the work.

We each got estimates and then came to mutual agreement on the work. The contractor alternated panels so one panel faced our yard and one faced his, which also made our fence much more resistant to damage as well. More than that, though, when all was said and done, we would periodically meet in our front yards, free of fences, and chat from time to time. That fence fell down and turned strangers into neighbors. This time, the true wisdom came in the proverb "Bad fences make good neighbors."

What fences have you put up in your life, and are they meant to keep people out or to bring people together?

Contextual Wisdom

These contrasting stories of neighbors and fences point to the value of the Proverbs. The proverbs for this lesson probably make us all squirm just a bit. They seem to be recommending that we act in generous and risky ways when it comes to being in relationship with other people and that we keep our guard up and not take such risks at the same time.

For example, "Don't say to your neighbor, 'Go, and come back; I'll give it to you tomorrow,' when you have it" (Proverbs 3:28). And in Proverbs 25:21, we read, "If your enemies are starving, feed them some bread; if they are thirsty, give them water to drink." But Proverbs 6:1-5 seems to discourage close interactions with neighbors, warning us against guaranteeing a loan for a neighbor and coming "under the control of [our] neighbor" due to an agreement (verse 3).

How can all those things be true?

Well, it is difficult for all of them to be true at all times and in all places. Part of what makes something wisdom is that it takes into account the context in which such advice is being offered. Proverbs implicitly recognizes that advice that may be true in X time at X place with X people may not be true in Y time at Y place with Y people. How do we know they recognized such variation?

We can look back to see how we are encouraged to be generous with our neighbors and our enemies, but also not to get too deeply involved with them as to guarantee a loan for them. Should we make such a mistake, apparently we should just drive our neighbor crazy until we can get out of it: "So go, humble yourself, and pester your neighbor"

(6:3). These passages seem less like encouraging us to be good neighbors just to show love to others and more like we should be good neighbors so we can get something out of it, or perhaps we should not be good neighbors at all.

The proverbs contradict other biblical wisdom from time to time. In fact, Proverbs contradicts Proverbs. Read Proverbs 26:4-5, two proverbs that contradict each other! Back to back! "Don't answer fools according to their folly, or you will become like them yourself. Answer fools according to their folly, or they will deem themselves wise."

It wasn't that the people who were pulling together the Bible somehow missed this fact. They recognized it. They just also recognized that the wise response in one situation could be the foolish response in another. It is how we can affirm the truth of these contradictory statements:

- Clothes make the person. You cannot judge a book by its cover.
- Familiarity breeds contempt. Home is where the heart is.
- Great minds think alike. Fools seldom differ.
- Laugh and the world laughs with you, but weep and you weep alone. Misery loves company.

It is also how I can say that good fences make good neighbors, good fences make bad neighbors, and bad fences make good neighbors. All of those are true. They just may not be true all at the same time.

Part of what makes someone wise is knowing when to use such wisdom and when to use something else. Our faith also calls us to make such judgments. Yes, we are to love our neighbors; but in doing so, as we follow Jesus as his disciples, we should, in his words, "be wise as snakes and innocent as doves" (Matthew 10:16). Showing love to others can be risky, but it is a risk God calls us to take.

When have you had to use a different approach than usual in order to be a faithful follower of God?

When We Couldn't Shake Hands

I have to admit, at the time I was writing this lesson (during quarantine due to the COVID-19 pandemic), I was shocked at the idea of shaking someone's hand. I cannot anticipate how we will all feel about this by the time you are reading this lesson. I can only sit in this moment when we have been told by medical personnel that perhaps the time of shaking anyone's hand has come to an end.

There is yet another example of context-shaping wisdom. If somehow we are all convinced that shaking hands is no longer a good idea, then the proverb warning us about shaking hands, which is intended to warn us off of making an unsavory financial deal, may shift in meaning to warn us about having unnecessary skin-to-skin contact with others.

Regardless, both meanings will be speaking to the risk involved in relating to others. In this moment, isolated in my home, I am acutely aware of the danger of contact with another human being. I have also never missed something so much in my life.

I took for granted having lunch with friends, hugging the people I love, even standing in line at the grocery store chatting with strangers. All of that has come to a halt, and my soul is withering on the vine from this isolation. It has nothing to do with being an introvert or an extrovert. It has to do with being human. It has to do with being created in the image of a triune God, a God who is one in three and united in perfect relationship. We are not meant for isolation. We are meant for communion and community.

One interesting side effect of this isolation, however, is that it has resulted in meeting so many of my neighbors.

We had all grown accustomed to our privacy fences, our houses with bigger backyard decks than front porches, our locked doors and security cameras. And now, hungry for contact with the outside world and desperate to get away from screens that are our only way of connecting with the people who live far from us, we are scattering into the streets to meet the people who live next door to us.

I have been thinking about how, for years now, the church has been teaching us to think in such bigger terms about loving our neighbors. With the accessibility of world-wide communications, we have encouraged people to think of the person living on the other side of the world as our neighbor.

While that is a good thing because it teaches us to love those who are different from us, I also wonder if it taught us to love without risk. There is little risk in loving poor people in Africa by sending mosquito nets to them. Yes, that is beautiful and saves lives and is a significant means of love. But those people from Africa will never show up on our doorstep and demand more from us.

The people right next door, however, they can be friends or foes. Those relationships require attention. Those relationships can be risky.

Years ago, my father thought he was doing the right thing by our neighbor by sharing what he learned about the property. Instead, the neighbor used that knowledge to bully us and to make us fearful of our own backyard. Our neighbor in Texas took a big risk in asking us to spend money on a fence he would like, but that resulted in a kindness between us. None of those reactions is predictable. People are infinitely variable. So are situations.

We are called to be wise. We are called to be innocent. And we are called to love our neighbors. That is risky.

Love is risky. We cannot control how such love is received. All we can do is try to love as wisely and kindly as we can.

Will that look different in different contexts? Absolutely. Will different people change the results? Yes. In fact, sometimes the same people will change the results. We still take the risk. We still love. So "don't withhold good from someone who deserves it, when it is your power to do so," the writer of Proverbs says (Proverbs 3:27). But remember that "singing a song to a troubled heart is like taking off a garment on a cold day or putting vinegar on a wound" (25:20). Be wise and discerning, but be loving and take risks.

The neighbor whose small patch of land was enclosed by our fence passed away. The family put the house up for sale, and a young couple purchased it. My father took a risk, and he went to the couple and explained the situation. He offered to pay a fair price for the land, and the couple gladly took it. They were grateful for my father's honesty. They were good neighbors to us from then on. Then the old adage was true. Good fences had finally made good neighbors.

When has loving your neighbor proved risky but you have done it anyway?

Lord, may we take the risks we need to take to love the people you have called us to love; in Jesus name we pray. Amen.

The Spiritual Practice of Studying and Applying Scripture

The legal expert asked Jesus what he needed to do to inherit eternal life, and Jesus asked the expert what the Scriptures told him to do. "You must love the Lord your God with all your heart, with all your being, with all your strength, and with all your mind, and love your neighbor as yourself, " he replied. So Jesus told the man to do that.

But then the legal expert asked, "But who is my neighbor?" So Jesus told him the story of the good Samaritan, who rescued the man who had been beaten and left for dead on the side of the road. When Jesus asked the expert who had been the neighbor, the man pointed to the Samaritan. Then Jesus told the expert, "Go and do likewise" (Luke 10:25-37).

This story not only teaches us that loving our neighbor is central to our faith, it also models for us another way of growing in our faith: studying and applying Scripture. For the legal expert and Jesus in this moment, the Scriptures were made of books from what we call the Old Testament. Of course, the New Testament didn't exist for Jesus and the expert at the time this encounter happened. Still, they show us first that it is important to know Scripture.

When the expert asked Jesus the key to eternal life, Jesus pointed the man to the Scriptures. The key is there. Thus, studying Scripture is central for understanding that journey. The Articles of Religion of the Methodist Church tell us that Scripture contains all things necessary for salvation. It appears Jesus agrees with us!

But Jesus and the expert did not stop there. They dug deeper. If salvation comes from loving God and neighbor, then who is my neighbor? Then Jesus shared a story to help illuminate that. But, finally, Jesus told the man to go and do just like the Samaritan.

It is not enough to know the stories. The stories must then also be put to action. The study of Scripture is key to our faith and salvation, but if we do not let it transform us and our world, we have missed the point. Both must go hand in hand.

Focal Passage: Ruth 2:4-16
Background Texts: Leviticus 19:18; Ruth 2:4-16; Matthew 19:16-22
Purpose Statement: To remember to care for the strangers in our land

Ruth 2:4-16

⁴Just then Boaz arrived from Bethlehem. He said to the harvesters, "May the LORD be with you."

And they said to him, "May the LORD bless you."

⁵Boaz said to his young man, the one who was overseeing the harvesters, "To whom does this young woman belong?"

⁶The young man who was overseeing the harvesters answered, "She's a young Moabite woman, the one who returned with Naomi from the territory of Moab. ⁷She said, 'Please let me glean so that I might gather up grain from among the bundles behind the harvesters.' She arrived and has been on her feet from the morning until now, and has sat down for only a moment."

⁸Boaz said to Ruth, "Haven't you understood, my daughter? Don't go glean in another field; don't go anywhere else. Instead, stay here with my young women. ⁹Keep your eyes on the field that they are harvesting and go along after them. I've ordered the young men not to assault you. Whenever you are thirsty, go to the jugs and drink from what the young men have filled."

[10]Then she bowed down, face to the ground, and replied to him, "How is it that I've found favor in your eyes, that you notice me? I'm an immigrant." [11]Boaz responded to her, "Everything that you did for your mother-in-law after your husband's death has been reported fully to me: how you left behind your father, your mother, and the land of your birth, and came to a people you hadn't known beforehand. [12]May the LORD reward you for your deed. May you receive a rich reward from the LORD, the God of Israel, under whose wings you've come to seek refuge." [13]She said, "May I continue to find favor in your eyes, sir, because you've comforted me and because you've spoken kindly to your female servant—even though I'm not one of your female servants."

[14]At mealtime Boaz said to her, "Come over here, eat some of the bread, and dip your piece in the vinegar." She sat alongside the harvesters, and he served roasted grain to her. She ate, was satisfied, and had leftovers. [15]Then she got up to glean.

Boaz ordered his young men, "Let her glean between the bundles, and don't humiliate her. [16]Also, pull out some from the bales for her and leave them behind for her to glean. And don't scold her."

Key Verse: "Then she got up to glean. Boaz ordered his young men, 'Let her glean between the bundles, and don't humiliate her'" (Ruth 2:15).

Christinah was accepted to come to the United States to study at a seminary and received a full scholarship. She was overjoyed to have this opportunity, and she knew it would allow her to have a broader understanding of the world and would make her a more effective pastor when she returned to her home country in Africa.

However, the conditions of Christinah's visa would not allow her to bring her 17-year-old daughter with her. She had family she could leave her daughter with, but she was worried. Her country was a dangerous one for young women.

It was a nervous first year of seminary. But as Christinah faced her second year, she was overjoyed to learn that her daughter had been accepted to study in a US university, and she had also received a full scholarship! So imagine her pain when she learned her daughter's visa was denied because her mother was already in the country. Mother and daughter were placed in vulnerable states, and a young woman stood to lose the opportunity to receive the education she needed to become a nurse and return to her home country with that knowledge and skill.

Christinah's story is one of thousands, each filled with hopes and dreams. Boaz heard Ruth's story, and that made all the difference. What other stories like these do we need to hear? How should we respond?

A 2016 resolution states in part, "United Methodists understand that 'at the center of Christian faithfulness to Scripture is the call we have been given to love and welcome the sojourner.'" The resolution further calls United Methodist churches to "welcome newly arriving migrants in their communities, to love them as we do ourselves, to treat them as one of our native-born, to see in them the presence of the incarnated Jesus, and to show hospitality to the migrants in our midst, believing that through their presence we are receiving the good news of the gospel of Jesus Christ."[1]

Bible on the Bus

When I served in Fort Smith, Arkansas, we took a couple of trips in the church van that I affectionately called "Bible on the Bus." We would take day trips to area sites of interest, and we would study something in the Bible related to the destination.

One of those trips involved going to Crystal Bridges, a renowned museum in Bentonville, Arkansas. The museum had a special exhibit of a photographer who had taken pictures of the debris left behind by people at the border wall between the United States and Mexico.

On the way up and back, we read and studied the Book of Ruth. Ruth was a stranger in a strange land. She had literally crossed into enemy territory. The tensions between the Moabites and the Israelites went back millennia, even though they traced common ancestry.

The area of the Moabites is what is now Jordan. To this day, you can see the division. When you dip into the Jordan River where Jesus was most likely baptized, on one side of the river are armed Jordanian soldiers. On the other side are armed Israelis. Time has not healed all wounds.

Bringing that Holy Land history in conversation with our current border reality, we couldn't help but feel the brokenness in our human family. The worn dolls abandoned as children fled for a new life, trying to remember our baptisms while people stood with guns aimed above us—it all seems so far from the vision God has for God's children.

I was grateful for the opportunity to look through the eyes of others, through the lens of the photographer at the museum and through the scope of the soldier in the Holy Land. Different perspectives are necessary if I am to continue to grow in my own faith and if I am to help others grow, too.

But even as we acknowledged the hopeful ideal, the discussion on the bus also named the real challenges. When is fear of the other justified, if ever? How do we remain a law-abiding society and still make room for love? It is not so cut-and-dried. Even when we consider the biblical position, we run into a variety of perspectives, which we can turn to now.

When have you had the opportunity to see a stranger's perspective, and how has it changed you?

The Biblical Witness(es)

One of the things that frustrates me when we study the Bible is that we are often not honest about how complicated the Bible is. I frequently tell my congregations or groups that I teach that I can use the Bible to justify any stance.

Partially that is due to the inherent flexibility of meaning found in practically any text. Partially, though, it is due to the fact that this one book is made up of many smaller books, books that represent different stages or contexts in different cultures' lives. When we look at complicated issues, such as immigration, characterizing the Bible as uniformly in favor of open borders is to be dishonest about the text.

Ruth's story is a good place to start when we consider just such an issue. Ruth was the daughter-in-law of Naomi, a woman from Judah who had relocated to Moab when there was a famine in Judah. She and her husband, Elimelech, had fled across the border to Moab because they could not provide for their family in their homeland.

While in Moab, things didn't go terribly well. Elimelech died, and then Naomi's two sons died, leaving behind a total of three widows: Naomi and her two daughters-in-law, Orpah and Ruth, who were both Moabite.

Naomi decided to return to her homeland, and Orpah went home to her family, but Ruth decided to go to Judah with her mother-in-law. Ruth was going where her family by marriage went, even if that was into hostile territory. (Moabites were not beloved by Israelites during most of their history.)

Now Ruth was a stranger in a strange land, and she had no way to care for herself and Naomi, except to go behind workers in the field and pick up their scraps. She did this in the field of a man named Boaz; and when Boaz found her, he told her to keep gleaning in his field and he would protect her. Then Ruth responded, "How is it that I've found favor in your eyes, that you notice me? I'm an immigrant" (Ruth 2:10).

The word in Hebrew Ruth used here to call herself an "immigrant" is *nakriyah* [knock-CREE], the feminine version of the word *nakriy*. That word caught my eye because it was not the word for "immigrant," "stranger," "alien," "foreigner" that I remembered learning in Hebrew. The word I learned was *geyr* [gare]. Having noticed the difference, I set about to see if there was a difference in connotation to the two words. There is.

Geyr tends to be used in situations in which an immigrant is viewed in positive or protective terms. In Exodus and Leviticus, it is used to describe strangers who are integrated into the community, as those who honor the Passover and fall under the same laws as the Israelites (for example, Exodus 12:49; Leviticus 17:10). It is the word for the protective laws given in Deuteronomy: "That means you must also love immigrants because you were immigrants in Egypt" (Deuteronomy 10:19). *Geyr* is a word of inclusion and assimilation.

But *nakriy* is used when there is a potential threat coming from strangers. It is a word reflecting fear and exploitation. It is the term Rachel and Leah used for how their father felt about them; they were just tools he could use to increase his wealth (Genesis 31:15). It was okay to call in a debt from a *nakriy*, but debts from fellow Israelites had to be forgiven in sabbatical years (Deuteronomy 15:13).

It is the root word that sometimes gets translated as "adulteress" in Proverbs. In prophets such as Obadiah, the foreigners were the ones who would come in and take land away from the Israelites (Obadiah 1:7). Then, most notably, it is the word used for foreigners in Ezra and Nehemiah.

Let's recall what was happening in Ezra–Nehemiah. The Israelite/Judean people had been given permission to leave their homes in exile and return to their homeland. Not only that, they could rebuild Jerusalem. These returning exiles arrived home to find other people living there. This would not do. If they were going to return to their past glory, and if they were going to recreate proper worship of God, they had to get rid of these foreign influences.

As a result, foreigners were cast out, including any foreign wives who had married Israelites/Judeans. Their children were also ousted. Then they set about to build a wall to keep those foreigners out. They had a culture to preserve, a way of life to defend, and there could be no threat to that project.

Into this division of meaning between *geyr* and *nakriy* came Ruth. Ruth's story is one of immigration driven by survival but also driven by love. But Ruth seems to have recognized what a precarious position she was in. She did not refer to herself as a *geyr* (someone who could expect to be included), but as *nakriyah* (someone who would be perceived as a threat). She was afraid. She was vulnerable.

She could be exploited. And Boaz would decide to what extent that would be the case. What was his response?

"Boaz responded to her, 'Everything that you did for your mother-in-law after your husband's death has been reported fully to me: how you left behind your father, your mother, and the land of your birth, and came to a people you hadn't known beforehand. May the LORD reward you for your deed. May you receive a rich reward from the LORD, the God of Israel, under whose wings you've come to seek refuge'" (Ruth 2:11-12).

Boaz knew Ruth's story. And as soon as he did, however he may have felt about immigrants beforehand, he had to make allowances for this woman who was just trying to survive and do right by her family.

Make no mistake, the tension between *geyr* and *nakriy* appears in the New Testament, though different words are used, and they tend to show up in the question of whether Gentiles are included in the family of God. So we have one biblical witness (in some Torah laws, in Ezra–Nehemiah, in the fears of the prophets, in the opponents of Paul) that calls for caution (or in more extreme cases, exploitation or deportation) when dealing with the stranger.

Then we have another witness (in some Torah laws, in the life witness of Jesus as he was an immigrant in Egypt and eventually includes Gentiles in the mission, and in Paul) that argues for inclusion and protection of the stranger. The Bible is not uniform in its stance toward the stranger, which means we are left to choose which biblical witness holds more authority with us.

Which biblical witnesses hold the most authority for you, and why?

Distinguishing Policy From People

In the midst of these legalistic debates wades the story of Ruth. Boaz learned of her story; and in that, there was a response of mercy and exception to the rule. And ultimately, this union created the path for the birth of David and eventually for the family of Jesus, both of whom are descendants of Ruth and Boaz.

Perhaps that is the lesson for us as we move across time and will continue to find ourselves caught between these two extremes in how we treat people. Maybe we should stop and hear one another's stories. Then we could understand better how a *nakriyah* could become a *geyr*, but also we could understand that there are many ways of seeing the world. The more we learn from one another, the more we are honest about the many sides of a story, and the more willing we are to hear one another's stories, the deeper our understanding of God's world will actually be.

Hearing stories also helps us distinguish between policy and people. When we heard the stories of children being kept in cages, regardless of political affiliations and commitments, many of us stood together in opposition to such treatment. Whether you want legal immigration strictly enforced or you want free movement of people fleeing oppression, few of us were on board with caging children. It took hearing the stories for us to get involved, however. That made the difference between focusing on people over policy.

MJ heard Christinah's story. For Christinah's first year in seminary, MJ was a kind ear. When MJ learned that Christinah's daughter was denied a chance at a quality education, however, MJ could no longer sit still. She also knew that Christinah was relatively powerless, but MJ, as an American citizen, was not. She began writing to congressmen and raising all sorts of a fuss.

Ultimately, she secured a visa for Christinah's daughter. Walking in life with her friend, she could see beyond the legal code to the young woman who had so much promise and could serve the world in meaningful ways.

In a similar way, Boaz paid attention to Ruth's story. He heard it for who she was, and thank God for that. He listened and loved, and ultimately Jesus Christ was born for us all.

When has knowing someone's story challenged how you understand our laws?

God of many stories, open our ears that we may hear and learn of the many lives of the people around us, and let that transform us into your family; in Jesus' name we pray. Amen.

[1]From *umc.org/en/content/ask-the-umc-what-is-the-united-methodist-position-on-immigration-reform.*

Focal Passage: Acts 6:1-7
Background Texts: Acts 2:36-42; 6:1-7; 9:26-31
Purpose Statement: To discern how the church can best care for its members in need

Acts 6:1-7

¹About that time, while the number of disciples continued to increase, a complaint arose. Greek-speaking disciples accused the Aramaic-speaking disciples because their widows were being overlooked in the daily food service. ²The Twelve called a meeting of all the disciples and said, "It isn't right for us to set aside proclamation of God's word in order to serve tables. ³Brothers and sisters, carefully choose seven well-respected men from among you. They must be well-respected and endowed by the Spirit with exceptional wisdom. We will put them in charge of this concern. ⁴As for us, we will devote ourselves to prayer and the service of proclaiming the word." ⁵This proposal pleased the entire community. They selected Stephen, a man endowed by the Holy Spirit with exceptional faith, Philip, Prochorus, Nicanor, Timon, Parmenas, and Nicolaus from Antioch, a convert to Judaism. ⁶The community presented these seven to the apostles, who prayed and laid their hands on them. ⁷God's word continued to grow. The number of disciples in Jerusalem increased significantly. Even a large group of priests embraced the faith.

Key Verse: "Brothers and sisters, carefully choose seven well-respected men from among you. They must be well-respected and endowed by the Spirit with exceptional wisdom. We will put them in charge of this concern" (Acts 6:3).

I have a nickname for my friend Cathy. I call her "Dinner Reservations." Cathy is one of those old-school masters of hospitality. She sets a beautiful table. She cooks amazing meals. She is particular about atmosphere. She makes certain the directions that will bring you to her table are impeccable, thus there is no chance that you will get lost.

But Cathy's hospitality extends beyond the details of an immaculate meal. Cathy pays attention. She sees what you need usually before you recognize it yourself. She listens deeply to your story and then brings representative pieces of who you are to the table. (For example, she adapts recipes to limit carbs or bakes your favorite flavor of cake or makes your own special dish to accommodate you.) She notices, and she notices well.

Cathy also gathers well. By that, I mean she has a knack for beating the bushes to find the people who are hungry for community. She is a good balance of reaching new people and caring for the ones who have been here a while.

But make no mistake, Cathy's work is primarily inside work. It is where she is comfortable and where she is gifted, and her goal is to bring everyone inside. Still, I suspect if Cathy were running things in the first century, no one would have been skipped in the meal service. Some people are beautifully cut of cloth that helps them see and make space for all kinds of people. I am grateful Cathy is one of those.

Perhaps Cathy is, in part, so good at including others at the table because she has sometimes been excluded from the table. She was a wild child tomboy growing up in a traditional Southern home, so she did not fit the cultural ideal around her much of her life. She has also been divorced, and sometimes the church is not the friendliest place for divorced people.

But the message of Scripture is clear: Everyone can have a seat at God's table. What do we need to do to ensure that each person feels welcomed, valued, and honored?

The Most Vulnerable Among Us

Sometimes we have to use our creative imagination to envision what the church of the first century looked like. We have good ideas that the church included rich and poor, Jews and Gentiles, men and women, and people who lived within and outside of Judea.

We do not know a whole lot more than that. We do know, though, that the early church definitely consisted of widows. Widows show up as part of the early church throughout the Book of Acts (see Acts 6 above and widows weeping for Tabitha in Acts 9) and in other biblical accounts, such as 1 Timothy 5.

We may have misconceptions about widows in the first century. There is a tendency to imagine that they were all destitute and fully dependent on the kindness of strangers to survive. That was certainly true for some widows and may have been the case for the widows here in Acts 6, since they seem to have been primary recipients of food service.

Widows could, however, control a significant amount of resources and seem to have been integral in funding much of the early Christian mission, including much of Jesus' ministry. Widows were the recipients of Jesus' compassion and healing on a number of occasions, such as the time he restored to life the only son of a widow in Nain (Luke 7:11-15). Jesus positively noted a widow for consistent prayer (Luke 18:1-8), something with which the New Testament associates widows (Luke 2:36-37; 1 Timothy 5:3-16). Jesus called attention to a widow's generosity (Mark 12:41-44; Luke 21:1-4) and strongly condemned the legal experts who appeared to be pious but "who [cheated] widows out of their homes" (Luke 20:47).

Unlike women in that culture who were married, widows were outside the bounds of being defined primarily by their relationship to a man and were typically more economically vulnerable than women who had husbands or who were still primarily cared for by their fathers.

However, Jewish women and Greek women could inherit (though at a lower percentage level than men in their family), and they could run their own businesses (Lydia in Acts 16, for example). In these cases, the women were less economically disadvantaged than they were socially so.

Because of Jesus' inclusion of women and Paul's value on the unmarried state, it appears that the early Christian communities may have been flooded with widows because they were welcomed and had purpose in the Christian community. So, the charge to distribute food to the Greek widows was not just a charge to take care of the most vulnerable. It may have been a charge to take care of the majority of those who belonged to the church.

As the church grew, that would, of course, become a more and more significant task, one that could not be managed by the leaders alone. The Christian community needed a division of labor if it was going to continue to grow. Why? Because one person could not and should not do this work alone.

Who are the most vulnerable among us today? How can the church best welcome and care for them?

Two Orders

Methodism has something somewhat unique. We have two ordained orders, and they do not exactly line up with any other denomination. This makes negotiations with other denominations to get full communion agreements (which include allowing pastors to serve in both denominations) a little tricky. However, our two orders arguably hearken to this moment in the early church when there was a distinct division of labor in church leadership.

The Methodist Church has ordained elders and ordained deacons. Both orders are called to Word and service, which means both can proclaim and teach the good news, and both can serve church and community. The difference comes in the other two traits of the orders.

Elders, typically the pastors of churches, are called to sacrament and order and are authorized to administer the sacraments in any context at any time. Elders are also called to order the church, which means paying attention to the administration and health of the local congregation and also committing to nurturing the denomination and the church universal. While elders care for the health of the congregation by growing it through interaction within the world, they tend to be understood as anchored in the church and then moving out into the world.

However, deacons might be best understood as serving in the world and bringing the world to the church. Deacons are ordained to compassion and justice. Again, that does not mean that elders don't engage in compassion and justice, but that deacons focus particularly on these.

A deacon's primary appointment tends to be in a secular role. Deacons serve as insurance agents, providing health and life insurance in an ethical manner, but also extending coverage to the poor and the marginalized. Deacons run nonprofits that address childhood illiteracy, head counseling centers, and teach elementary or high school. Deacons work with the homeless on the streets and with addicts in recovery. They do have a secondary appointment to a local congregation, which is how they keep their mission in conversation with the church.

This moment in the early church we find in Acts 6 was the division of labor. It recognized that the work of the church cannot be left solely to the administrators. It is the work of all the people. Still, the temptation to leave it to the professionals is a strong one. What happens to our ability to care for the community when we professionalize the work of the church too much?

Why do you think it is important to distinguish between the work of deacons and elders in The Methodist Church?

Not a One-Person Show

Seven weeks into the COVID-19 quarantine, we witnessed a miracle. In the span of one week (the first week of the quarantine), the church went online en masse, effectively jumping from the twentieth to the twenty-first century overnight. It was absolutely incredible to watch, and I will forever be in awe of my clergy colleagues who essentially learned a whole new bag of tricks for sharing the gospel virtually (pardon the pun) overnight.

With the quarantine in full effect, however, pastors struggled to find ways to easily integrate laity into helping them with the production of worship. In my particular state, due to some spotty internet access, it became clear that many of our churches needed to prerecord worship and load it to premiere on Sunday morning.

For pastors, that meant that their workload tripled. Because these worship services had some amount of permanence, and because they could edit them, pastors were sometimes filming multiple takes. Then there was the vast amount of editing. Then came the formatting and the uploading, and they still had to plan out worship and line out music.

What had been a three- to four-hour process to plan and execute worship (not counting sermon prep) was now taking days. And without the ability to sit down with their laity, they could not train them to help with all these tasks, even though some laity were probably more ready for such work than pastors were.

The result was that other pastoral tasks, such as the now personal necessity of calling every single parishioner to check on them, started to seriously slip. But that was the thing. Calling and checking on people, that didn't require any training. That just required an updated directory (which, admittedly, was still something of a challenge for some).

A necessary division of labor had to occur, otherwise people were going to go unattended for potentially weeks, damaging the mission and connection of the community. So some were appointed to carry out that important work of making sure everyone was cared for.

This moment was not terribly unlike the situation faced here in Acts. The professional leaders of the faith community had obviously become overextended. They had to oversee worship. Care of the broader community, however, could and should be shared. The lesson learned in the first century is a lesson we are learning again in the twent-first century. We do not need for professional clergy to do everything in the church. It damages our witness and our viability. However, if we share the load and authorize others to share in the care, then so much more good can happen.

Is the work of your church effectively spread among clergy and laity? How can volunteers help so that pastors have more time to devote to tasks that only they can do?

Will Call

Jesus had designated certain people to be apostles, distinct from the crowd of disciples (for example, Luke 6:12-16). Did the church subsequently understand that to mean that apostles were meant to do the work of the church and everyone else should just follow? Perhaps that was how the church had been operating, but in this moment, it became clear that such an approach would not work as the church grew. Others would need to share their gifts to take some roles in the church.

Notice how they went about making this decision. They asked for discernment of seven men who were well-respected and had the spiritual gift of wisdom. Does that seem odd? We might have expected that for table service they would look for people with the gift of hospitality, or at the very least were good cooks and organizers. But, no, they wanted men who were well-respected and wise. Why? What were these men actually managing?

It was less the distribution of food and more the unrest in the community. If the community came apart at this critical juncture in the church's history, who knows what might happen to the future of the proclamation of the gospel!

Not only do we all have different spiritual gifts, but we also have distinct understandings for how we live out our discipleship. In my personal study, I developed a framework for understanding our discipleship in terms of the four Gospels and a test to help people determine how they understand discipleship. (For more information, see *gospel discipleship.net*.).

Acts is part of the Lukan understanding of discipleship, and Lukans grow in their discipleship through the relationships they cultivate. Is it any wonder, then, that Lukan discipleship would center around table inclusion and that preservation of the community through appointing the wise ones to navigate through difficult waters would be so important?

The Spirit will call forward and gift the community to fulfill the needs it has. Just like the Spirit has gifted me to order the church and has gifted Cathy, who is a lay person, to care for the body within the church, the Spirit knows who can thrive in what space. The division of labor allows for the expansion of our capacity to be the church, which consequently expands our witness. The Spirit gifts the community to care for its own, and the Spirit gifts the community to reach out and expand its reach.

What we have to do is recognize who is gifted for which type of movement at which time. Both are critical to the mission of the church. Let's be intentional about putting the right people in place for each mission so that the work of the Spirit is unleashed.

Do you personally feel more strongly called to care for those within your church or reach new people to grow your church? How are you living into that call?

Lord, may we have the strength to live more fully as a church into caring for our own and reaching new ones in your name; in Jesus' name we pray. Amen.

Focal Passage: Mark 2:1-12
Background Texts: Matthew 9:1-8; Mark 2:1-12; Luke 5:17-26
Purpose Statement: To marvel at how invested true neighbors are with one another

Mark 2:1-12

¹After a few days, Jesus went back to Capernaum, and people heard that he was at home. ²So many gathered that there was no longer space, not even near the door. Jesus was speaking the word to them. ³Some people arrived, and four of them were bringing to him a man who was paralyzed. ⁴They couldn't carry him through the crowd, so they tore off part of the roof above where Jesus was. When they had made an opening, they lowered the mat on which the paralyzed man was lying. ⁵When Jesus saw their faith, he said to the paralytic, "Child, your sins are forgiven!"

⁶Some legal experts were sitting there, muttering among themselves, ⁷"Why does he speak this way? He's insulting God. Only the one God can forgive sins."

⁸Jesus immediately recognized what they were discussing, and he said to them, "Why do you fill your minds with these questions? ⁹Which is easier—to say to a paralyzed person, 'Your sins are forgiven,' or to say, 'Get up, take up your bed, and walk'? ¹⁰But so

you will know that the Human One has authority on the earth to forgive sins"—he said to the man who was paralyzed, [11]"Get up, take your mat, and go home."

[12]Jesus raised him up, and right away he picked up his mat and walked out in front of everybody. They were all amazed and praised God, saying, "We've never seen anything like this!"

Key Verses: "Some people arrived, and four of them were bringing to him a man who was paralyzed. They couldn't carry him through the crowd, so they tore off part of the roof above where Jesus was. When they had made an opening, they lowered the mat on which the paralyzed man was lying" (Mark 2:3-4).

The family insisted that their mother's neighbor Debbie sit with them on the first pew during the funeral. She was to be considered as close as any family member could be. She was listed in the obituary as one of the survivors, all because one day, Debbie looked over her fence, noticed an older woman next door, and decided to strike up a conversation.

Debbie and Carol became fast friends, even though 30 years of age separated them. As Carol grew more frail, Debbie grew more attentive. She took dinner to Carol every night for a while, and then it was dinner and breakfast. She went to the store for Carol. She drove her to doctor's appointments. She dug the grave for Carol's beloved cat.

Then, as Carol's mind started slipping, Debbie grew concerned that Carol was not safe in the house alone. She talked with the family and made her offer. She could move into the house with Carol. The family had nothing to fear from this offer because they had watched Debbie love their mother for years. So she moved in, and she was there for that last night, standing in vigil with all the family, when Carol took her last breath.

The family was at peace in the passing of their mother, but collectively they worried deeply about Debbie. They knew her loss was great. She had lost a friend, and she had lost a purpose. Her purpose had been to love her neighbor.

Humans seem to have a knack for creating architecture that barricades us from other people. A fence might have kept Debbie and Carol apart, and they might have missed a friendship of a lifetime. Similarly, the friends of the paralyzed man we read about in Mark 2 might have been discouraged by architecture. A house packed full of people and walls and a roof keeping them out. They might have said, "Oh, well. No way to get to Jesus today. Sorry, friend."

But the architecture didn't stop them, just as it didn't stop Debbie from talking to her neighbor.

Peeking Over Fences, Tearing Down Roofs

During the time of Jesus, the roofs of homes in that area were made of thatch that had to be replaced periodically. To make that process easier, small steps up the sides of houses allowed people to climb up and work on their roofs. Still, those steps were only wide enough for one foot in front of the other.

A group of people carrying another person up those steps would have been challenging. But these friends were up for that challenge. They were determined to take their friend to Jesus. Not only that, it is probably safe to assume that this house was not theirs. It is a pretty bold move to tear the roof off someone else's house, even if it is relatively easy to replace, all the bolder to then lower someone down through the roof to reach Jesus!

We encounter barriers among ourselves and our neighbors. We also encounter barriers in bringing our neighbors to Jesus. Sometimes that barrier is busyness. Sometimes it is fear. Sometimes it is concern about the commitment it would take to carry them there. Sometimes it is feelings of inadequacy: How can I bring someone to Jesus when my own life feels like such a mess?

Then there are the barriers of a church that "looks too fancy" for people, that intimidates them from going in the doors. All of those are obstacles. But a bold faith looks for ways to scale the walls, to tear off the roof, to bring people to Jesus. As we grow in our passion for Christ, we become more creative and determined in our desire to connect others to Jesus, and more of those obstacles come down.

What obstacles are keeping you from bringing your neighbors to Jesus, and what would it take to overcome them?

Whose Faith?

This passage includes interesting details that are sometimes overshadowed by the dramatic roof removal and then the healing that led to a paralyzed man walking. However, these details are at the heart of the call on our lives to love our neighbors. They are profound acts of love that transform the reality before everyone.

We do notice that it was four friends who carried this man to Jesus and lowered him through the roof. "There was no longer space" in the house, "not even near the door" (Mark 2:2). They "couldn't carry him through the crowd, so they tore off part of the roof above where Jesus was" (verse 4).

But do we notice that it was their faith that prompted Jesus to extend forgiveness to the paralyzed man? Stop for just a minute, and think about what this says. "When Jesus saw their faith, he said to the paralytic, 'Child, your sins are *forgiven!*'" (verse 5; italics added).

As far as we know, the paralyzed man did not ask for forgiveness, but the faith of his friends prompted Jesus to offer it anyway. The implications, then, are that if people take measures to bring someone before Jesus, then whether they can voice their need or not, Jesus will meet it.

Can we see what the Scripture is saying there? Do you know what this means? Our faith, our willingness to kneel at the altar and bring someone else there to Jesus, can lead to forgiveness. Our love as neighbors can reconcile people to Christ!

Perhaps your heart is currently heavy because of someone who needs to be reconciled to Jesus. Perhaps this is someone who seems too broken to get to the point of reconciliation themselves. According to this Scripture, it is enough that you are bold enough to tear off the roof and bring them to the feet of Christ. Your faith can lead to their forgiveness. Your faith!

Who do you need to bring boldly before Christ to help lead him or her to forgiveness and reconciliation?

A Healing Witness

The next detail underscores that it is the actions of those of us who have encountered the power of Christ, who then bring others to faith. After Jesus forgave the paralyzed man, "some legal experts were sitting there, muttering among themselves, 'Why does he speak this way? He's insulting God. Only the one God can forgive sins'" (Mark 2:6-7).

In contrast to the faith of the friends, Jesus encountered doubters (who were all taking up space from people who were trying to get to Jesus because they did believe). So Jesus' response was to heal the paralyzed man and ask him to stand up. "Get up, take your mat, and go home" (verse 11).

Now, that man had options. He could have stayed on his mat and said, "I don't know what you are talking about, Jesus." He was taking a risk insulting and embarrassing the powers that be if he stood up. So now, it was his turn to do something bold to transform the faith of others. When he stood up, he showed people who Jesus is. "They were all amazed and praised God, saying, 'We've never seen anything like this!'" (verse 12)

It is possible that the man did not go there to be healed of his paralysis. After all, that is not what Jesus extended to him at first. Jesus gave him forgiveness. But then, in order to open up others to the power of Christ, he had to change his life and then demonstrate that change to others. So the other piece of love of neighbor that we see in this passage is that those who know the power of Christ in our lives need to be willing to show others how that changes us.

We need to be willing to stand up and take our mat, even if that means we can't stay where we are comfortable. We have to love Christ and others enough to change, and we have to be willing to publicly demonstrate that change in our lives, too.

The line at the pharmacy always seems to take longer than I want it to take. One day, a woman in front of me was not only picking up her prescriptions, but she was also picking up the prescriptions of her neighbor. That meant she was paying separately. She paid for hers, and then the pharmacist rang up her neighbor's bill. To her surprise, it came to $60. Her neighbor had given her $20 and told her he knew it would cover most but not all of it. She was prepared to contribute another $20, but $40 had flustered her.

I reached in my purse and handed the pharmacist $20. She said, "Oh, no. You shouldn't have to do that."

"Nonsense," I said. "I am happy to do it. After all, we are all neighbors, right?" And that was the opportunity I missed.

While I did love my neighbor—and to some extent, I had been bold—I did not tie it to my faith. It was not evident that Christ had transformed my life into a person who would not hesitate to pay for the medicine for a stranger. I could have easily said, "Jesus Christ calls me to love my neighbor. Your neighbor is my neighbor. And you are my neighbor, too." I missed my chance to pick up my mat and walk.

How can you witness to how Christ has transformed your life?

Love Your Neighbor

Jesus said that the two greatest commandments are to love God and to love neighbor (Matthew 22:37-39; Mark 12:30-31; Luke 10:27). This event we read from Mark, which we also find in Matthew 9:1-8 and Luke 5:17-26 (Matthew's version minus a few details), shares the story of friends who loved their neighbor enough to take him to Christ. They were his hands and feet. They were the wings of eagles that carried him to heights and then lowered him down. They did not see limitations to what they could do for their friend.

Debbie did not see the fence between her house and Carol's as a limitation either. She looked past the fence to see the woman on the other side. She saw the chance to meet Carol where she was, to walk alongside her, to love her to the end.

Are these two examples of extraordinary love? Maybe. But maybe they seem extraordinary only because we do not always take Jesus' words seriously. We have opportunities to show love all around us all the time. How often do we take the opportunity to respond the way Jesus calls us to love?

Of course, the other piece of the puzzle is that our neighbors have to be willing to be loved. Certainly, we can love them without their permission. We can love anyone we want. Expressing that love, however, involves the willing reception of that love. That response is the piece of the equation that we cannot control.

We also cannot control what our neighbors do with our love. That is not our responsibility, however. As followers of Christ, our responsibility and our call are to love our neighbors. What our neighbors do with that love is between them and God. We hope that they are transformed, that they learn to walk in new ways. But ultimately, that is their choice, not ours.

As we acknowledged in a previous lesson, there is risk in loving our neighbors. That continues to be true. But there is also great reward. The depths of these relationships can sustain us beyond the bonds of family. And they can witness to the world what a life following Christ can do: lead to love abundant and love beyond obstacles.

When have you loved a neighbor in a way that would be pleasing to Christ?

Friend Jesus, help us to love without limits and to boldly tear down obstacles that keep our neighbors from you; in Jesus' name we pray. Amen.

Daily Bible Readings (Unit 3)

July 26
Psalm 3:1-8

July 27
Numbers 22:20-35

July 28
1 Chronicles
21:1-8

July 29
Zechariah 3:1-10

July 30
Job 1:1-5

July 31
Job 1:6-12

August 1
Job 1:13-20

August 2
Psalm 139:19-24

August 3
1 Samuel 3:10-21

August 4
John 18:1-11

August 5
Acts 21:1-14

August 6
Job 1:21-22

August 7
Job 2:1-6

August 8
Job 2:7-10

August 9
Psalm 43:1-5

August 10
Job 2:11-13

August 11
Job 4:1-9

August 12
Job 11:13–12:5

August 13
Job 19:1-6

August 14
Job 19:7-19

August 15
Job 19:20-27

August 16
Psalm 44:9-26

August 17
Job 7:1-10

August 18
Job 7:11-15

August 19
Job 30:1-8

August 20
Job 30:9-15

August 21
Job 30:16-23

August 22
Job 30:24-31

August 23
Psalm 13:1-6

August 24
Job 38:1-14

August 25
Job 38:25-38

August 26
Job 40:1-14

August 27
Job 41:1-10

August 28
Job 42:1-6

August 29
Job 42:7-17

Unit 3
The Five Stages of Job

Siddhartha Gautama was a prince who had only known a life of ease in the palace where he lived in Nepal. When he started leaving the palace, however, he encountered people who were sick and dying and suffering greatly. He began a lifelong quest to confront and then transcend suffering. He left his palatial life and lived as a holy man. You might know him as the one referred to as the Buddha.

Buddha was trying to find a solution to the question of theodicy. Basically, it boils down to this: Why does God permit evil and suffering in the world? Where is God's justice in the midst of such pain? Humanity has been wrestling with this question as long as we have tried to make sense of our existence. We have particularly struggled with the idea of a good and loving God who oversees a world where so much struggle takes place. How can the two things be held together?

The Book of Job is the biblical book that deeply wrestles with this question. Here was a good man, a righteous man, one who was attentive to God and family, and who seems to have prospered in that reality as well. Then suddenly, everything was lost. Had he fallen out of God's favor? Did he have a secret sin he wasn't owning up to? Come on, Job, what did you do? These are the not-so-helpful responses he received from his friends. As unhelpful as they were, they did give voice to things that people say to us when we are suffering or to the questions we ask ourselves when we suffer.

Still, in this unit of lessons, we will not focus on those responses. Instead, we will focus on the experience of suffering. We will raise some of those same questions, but we will do so in light of few good answers in the face of the pain experienced. Ultimately, though, we will end in the whirlwind, which is the answer our faith gives us. No, we may not transcend suffering in this lifetime, we will not find that faith makes us bulletproof to life, but we can be confident in this: God knows our suffering and will show up in it. Always.

Focal Passage: Job 1:8-20
Background Texts: Job 1:1-20; Psalm 3:1-8
Purpose Statement: To reclaim lament as integral to worship

Job 1:8-20

[8] The LORD said to the Adversary, "Have you thought about my servant Job; surely there is no one like him on earth, a man who is honest, who is of absolute integrity, who reveres God and avoids evil?"

[9] The Adversary answered the LORD, "Does Job revere God for nothing? [10] Haven't you fenced him in—his house and all he has—and blessed the work of his hands so that his possessions extend throughout the earth? [11] But stretch out your hand and strike all he has. He will certainly curse you to your face."

[12] The LORD said to the Adversary, "Look, all he has is within your power; only don't stretch out your hand against him." So the Adversary left the LORD's presence.

[13] One day Job's sons and daughters were eating and drinking wine in their oldest brother's house. [14] A messenger came to Job and said: "The oxen were plowing, and the donkeys were grazing nearby [15] when the

Sabeans took them and killed the young men with swords. I alone escaped to tell you."

¹⁶While this messenger was speaking, another arrived and said: "A raging fire fell from the sky and burned up the sheep and devoured the young men. I alone escaped to tell you."

¹⁷While this messenger was speaking, another arrived and said: "Chaldeans set up three companies, raided the camels and took them, killing the young men with swords. I alone escaped to tell you."

¹⁸While this messenger was speaking, another arrived and said: "Your sons and your daughters were eating and drinking wine in their oldest brother's house, ¹⁹when a strong wind came from the desert and struck the four corners of the house. It fell upon the young people, and they died. I alone escaped to tell you."

²⁰Job arose, tore his clothes, shaved his head, fell to the ground, and worshipped.

Key Verse: "Job arose, tore his clothes, shaved his head, fell to the ground, and worshipped" (Job 1:20).

It started just after lunch that day. The morning had been a fairly benign day of ministry. A few people came in needing assistance. I had answered some emails and done a little writing; but that afternoon, things took a definite turn. Four people, none of whom had an appointment, walked in, each with a different story. Each story got worse.

The last story was a tale of abuse that would turn the stomach of anyone, except apparently the person who was inflicting the abuse. The one who was sharing the story, however, was an observer. So the hands of both of us were tied. Neither of us could step in as abuser and abused were competent adults. To call the police would put the one being abused in significant danger, perhaps before she was ready to leave.

When that last person left my office, I looked at the ceiling, as we sometimes do when we feel as if we need to look straight at God. "Is this some kind of wager you and Satan have made, God? Are you trying to see if I will quit the ministry? Are you sending worse and worse stories to get me to give up? Well, I tell you what, I am not quitting!" It was the end of the day. I stood up, packed my backpack, went home, ate cookies for dinner, and went to bed. Tomorrow would be another day.

No one gets through life without days like this. Even more poignant, however, practically no one gets through life without suffering the way the people who came in my office that day described. It is this universal experience of suffering that makes Job so compelling. Job asked the questions we all tend to ask in such experiences, questions of theodicy: Where is God's justice in the midst of such unjust and difficult times?

In the midst of tragedy upon tragedy, in the midst of incomparable grief, Job did what we all would do. Job lamented, but Job also worshiped.

Setting the Stage: Background on Job

Job may contain some of the oldest writings in the Bible. The prologue and the epilogue (Job 1:1–2:11;

42:7-17) not only are written in prose and not in poetry like the rest of the book, they also seem to participate in an older tradition about a legendary figure from antiquity named Job who was renowned for his righteousness. Ezekiel 14:14, 20 refers to Job, but there is debate as to whether Ezekiel was referring to the story recounted in our biblical text or if he was making reference to other tradition around Job.

Because of an apparent legend of Job in the ancient Near East and the switch in genre of literature, it may be that the Book of Job that we have before us now is an assembly of multiple traditions about Job. If that is the case, the prologue and the epilogue are probably the older pieces of the book and may date anywhere from the tenth to the seventh century BC. Most likely, the book itself was pulled together during the Exile in the sixth century, when the themes of the book would resonate with the people.

The prologue introduces three central characters. We have already mentioned Job and his legendary status. Most of the lessons in this unit will unpack the character of another central figure, God. The remaining character, translated in the CEB as "the Adversary," calls for a bit of reflection here.

The Hebrew word for "Adversary" is *Ha-Satan*. This is where we get the name *Satan*. The age of this book makes this likely the first appearance of Satan in the Bible. (Satan does not appear in Genesis 3; that character is a serpent. Only later interpretations link the two.) It is important, however, to notice who Ha-Satan actually is and isn't here.

This is not the horned and hoofed fiery ruler of hell so many of us picture when we hear the word *Satan*. Instead, Ha-Satan was a member of this court of God. The role Ha-Satan actually played is well caught in the translation as the Adversary.

Ha-Satan played the prosecuting attorney, bringing charges and challenges before God about Job. Like a prosecuting attorney bringing charges against a man, the Adversary literally was given power over Job's movement and prosperity. As a member of the court of justice, the Adversary was given enormous freedom to be unjust, but given that freedom with the permission of God. That frame will create much of the tension for us as we wrestle with the unfolding of this story.

One more interesting detail on the background of Job. You have probably heard reference to the patience of Job, and that reference is supposed to actually represent someone who is patient. But as we read the Book of Job, we discover that Job was not terribly patient. Where did that expression come from then? James 5:11 reads, "Look at how we honor those who have practiced endurance. You have heard of the endurance of Job."

Endurance is not necessarily the same thing as patience, but they are related. There was also a Testament of Job produced somewhere between the first century BC and the first century AD that takes the rabbinic approach popular at that time that did emphasize Job's patience. Job never yelled at God in the recounting of his story to his family in that work. The same cannot be said of Job in our biblical book. Job brought his anguish before God and leveled charges of injustice at God's feet.

What have you learned about the Book of Job that interested you? What other questions do you have about this book?

About Those Drive-Through Funeral Homes

As Job's story unfolds, we read that Job repeatedly wished for his own death. He was impatient, but he had a right to be. He was also suffering, so he responded with lament.

But Job's response may make us uncomfortable. Why? Perhaps because we are uncomfortable with the questions it raises about God, and we will certainly work through that over the course of the next four lessons. But perhaps we are also uncomfortable with lament. Perhaps we have lost an appreciation for this ritual expression of grief. Perhaps we are just uncomfortable with grief.

Have you heard of or perhaps seen a drive-through funeral home? During the set visitation time, the casket is pushed up against an outside window, people drive up in their cars to the window, and they pay their respects.

My reaction to drive-through funeral homes is the same as my reaction to people who think we should not pull over for funeral processions anymore. Ours is a culture uncomfortable with loss. Many people no longer make time for mourning. They do not make the time to cry, to moan, and to let their hearts ache anymore. It makes me want to quote Emily Dickinson: "Because I could not stop for Death, he kindly stopped for me."

This is in stark contrast to the expectations of the ancient world, where lament was not only a ritual expectation, it was a career. Professional mourners accompanied funerals, wailing and expressing grief at loss. Lament also shows up in ancient literature, including the poetry of Sumeria dating from 4,000 years ago. As long as people have been feeling, we have been expressing grief. And as long as we have experienced the loss of ones we have loved and recognized that through ritual response (funerals, for example), lament has been part of our worship.

In the Western world, however, many people tend to view grief in some ways as a failure. They tell themselves, wrongly, that they ought to be tougher than this. They also put a greater value, at least in the United States, on things that are new and shiny rather than old and showing wear.

So grief seems contrary to many of our dearly held values. But we can value all those things together and just recognize that different moments in life call for different responses.

We need to reclaim value in lament in worship, beyond the occasional expression in funerals and on All Saints Sunday. But when and how should we do so? Perhaps the answer lies in the journey of grief itself.

What other elements of our society reveal that we are uncomfortable expressing grief and loss?

Lament: Immediate and Delayed

Job 1:13-19 describes a series of four messengers who went to Job to tell him about loss after loss of livestock, young men tending them, and Job's sons and daughters. Job's response to his loss was sudden: "Job arose, tore his clothes, shaved his head, fell to the ground, and worshipped" (Job 1:20).

The grief was immediate and overwhelming, and it should have been. Because Job was a man who kept his faith practices at the center of his life, he needed that ritual expression right then. He fell down and worshiped.

The Book of Job also ends with Job worshiping. In that case, Job's friends were required by God to bring offerings to apologize for how poorly they represented God when they were trying to be present for Job, and Job offered prayers on their behalf. There is certainly much to unpack about God's expectations there. But for our purposes here, we will just note that ritual also occurs on the back side of the hard times.

Both ritual moments are important. They should be defined less by a particular timeline, though, and more by how the grief unfolds. That means paying attention to the moments. So when we think about ritual grief, we need to be open to immediate response that may disrupt other plans, and we need to plan for later responses that allow the grief that has changed and has a different purpose to still be expressed.

This moment in time has me reflecting on two rituals of lament, one I experienced long ago and one I eagerly await experiencing. The first took place in the immediate aftermath of the September 11 terrorist attacks. It was the first major event I had experienced as someone who went to church. I do not know a single pastor who did not change her or his sermon that following Sunday. Expressions of lament and cries of injustice and mourning were shared across the nation.

But the lament did not stop there. It continued deeply into the year. It came in waves. It came as we stopped the rescue effort and moved to recovery. It came as our communities felt the economic impact and people lost jobs. It came as we faced going to war. Lament unfolded. It continues to unfold. I was seven years away from serving as a pastor when the towers came down, but I have certainly taken time as a pastor for us to express lament, if only in abbreviated form.

The moment I anxiously await at this writing is our return to worship as we come out of the Covid-19 quarantine. I fear there will be a rush, considering our drive-through funeral home culture, to jump right to celebration and skip over lament. But we do ourselves a psychological and spiritual disservice if we do not take time to ritually mourn what we have lost.

We have lost old ways of doing things; and in some cases, we have literally lost people. If we do not stop to acknowledge that and bring it before God, we will miss a crucial step in our process of healing from it. We cannot move forward on the new if we do not recognize, honor, and memorialize what came before. And we need to stop and wail at what is gone so we can know what foundation we stand on going forward.

We will also need to return to reflection in later days when we can look back and learn from what all we have experienced in these moments. Lament needs to show up in the immediate aftermath, and we need to return to naming our struggles later, too, when we have had the time to reflect on how we have been shaped by loss.

When have you lamented in your life?

Reclaiming the Ritual Expression of Grief

It is striking that Job's response was worship. But then we are told that Job worshiped regularly, particularly to protect the souls of his children.

Job 1:5 tells us, "When the days of the feast had been completed, Job would send word and purify his children. Getting up early in the morning, he prepared entirely burned offerings for each one of them, for Job thought, Perhaps my children have sinned and then cursed God in their hearts. Job did this regularly." Job had so completely integrated worship in his life that it was his default response when he had deep soul cries he needed to express.

Do we make space for people to be so honest in our worship? Is worship so true to who our people are that it is the go-to response in times of celebration and desolation? I would love to be able to answer yes to this question, but I don't think it would be honest.

Perhaps the reason we do not fall suddenly to our knees and worship in such moments is because worship does not always adequately express the depth of human experience. It is time-consuming to plan an entirely new worship experience each week. It is easier to just stick to the tried-and-true patterns of worship and stay surface-level in content because diving deep opens cans of worms.

There is some comfort in predictable worship, and in some ways it mirrors the everyday nature of life. But too much of that flattens out worship and does not reflect the breadth of human experience. Then it fails to connect with us.

If worship does not provide space for all the messiness of life, it is inauthentic. We are supposed to bring all of who we are to God. That is what it means to be a whole and living sacrifice. If we are giving ourselves over to God in worship, then we need to give our whole selves over.

Yes, that includes our hope and joy, but that also includes our mess. That includes our loss. That includes our grief. That includes our anger. If the Book of Job teaches us anything, it affirms for us that God wants us to bring ourselves before God, honestly offering who we are. And when we do, that's when we will encounter God.

When have you experienced lament in worship? When do you think we have missed an opportunity to ritually lament?

Lord, we are grateful that you are the kind of God who will hear our cries, the kind of God who takes our authentic pain and transforms it into depth of connection. Thank you; in Jesus' name we pray. Amen.

The Spiritual Practice of Lament

"If one more person suggests to me that I should pray the Psalms, I may punch them in the face." That was probably as good a proof as any that I needed to be praying the Psalms.

I was in one of those "dark nights of the soul" when I felt deeply disconnected from God. I could not form the words. Actually, if I am honest, I didn't want to talk to God. Really, what could God say to me anyway that would make me feel better? No, I needed things fixed, and God wasn't going to do that, so what was there to talk about?

Sometimes we don't have the words. Sometimes we have too many words, and sometimes those words are not clean and pretty. They are backed by rage. They are backed by hurt. They are backed by complete sadness. They don't feel like words we should bring to God, which is exactly why we should bring them to God. I sometimes tell people, "Go ahead. Yell at God. God can take it." But getting up the nerve to do that—sometimes that takes a bit.

We see that happen in Job. Job starts out calmly sitting through his loss, praising God and affirming God's goodness. As the loss and time goes on, however, Job gets less and less nice. He starts to moan and bewail his own state and then to criticize and taunt God. The gloves are coming off as this book goes further along, and Job is naming that reality right to the ear of God.

There is something to be said for praying the Psalms, and particularly the psalms of lament. They give us the words we sometimes can't muster. But they also let us join the chorus of humanity. We all suffer. We all ache. And we all need to name that reality to God. When we do it together, we feel that much less alone.

Focal Passages: Job 1:21-22; 2:7-10
Background Texts: Job 1:21-22; 2:1-10; Psalm 139:19-24
Purpose Statement: To evaluate our willingness to "let God be God"

Job 1:21-22

²¹He said: "Naked I came from my mother's womb; naked I will return there. The LORD has given; the LORD has taken; bless the LORD's name." ²²In all this, Job didn't sin or blame God.

Job 2:7-10

⁷The Adversary departed from the LORD's presence and struck Job with severe sores from the sole of his foot to the top of his head. ⁸Job took a piece of broken pottery to scratch himself and sat down on a mound of ashes. ⁹Job's wife said to him, "Are you still clinging to your integrity? Curse God, and die."

¹⁰Job said to her, "You're talking like a foolish woman. Will we receive good from God but not also receive bad?" In all this, Job didn't sin with his lips.

Key Verse: "[Job] said: 'Naked I came from my mother's womb; naked I will return there. The LORD has given; the LORD has taken; bless the LORD name.'" (Job 1:21).

Blisters. All over my two-month-old's body. They had started out as just red patches. The pediatrician initially thought they were stork bites, those birth marks that show up on a newborn's skin. But, no, now they were blistered.

First guess was warts, which is not terribly comforting to a new mother. But then they started swelling and bursting open. Our doctor was mystified, so he called in his entire staff to look at my child's skin. No guesses.

We were referred to a dermatologist. The first one would not be able to work us in for seven months! The next one could see us in a month—a month! I would have a newborn child with blisters who would just have to suffer in his state for a month! He was fussy, with good reason, and my husband and I were stressed.

When we finally got in, the dermatologist, who had done a stint at Arkansas Children's Hospital, took one look and said, "Well, that's clearly urticaria pigmentosa." Clearly. What it meant for us was that we would have a child who would confront a myriad of contact allergies, and our lives would be significantly altered as we made space to keep him from suffering. In the midst of the whirlwind of reconfiguring our ways of being, I had to look toward God. But often I was looking to ask, "Really, God?!?!? Why my child?"

I have a pretty robust theology around suffering. Part of it comes from ten years of professional theological schooling. More of it, though, comes from a life lived. This theology affirms that God does not inflict evil on us, that God is indeed loving and good and seeks lives of thriving for all of us. That being said, when things come crashing down, I don't always keep that robust theology in the forefront. Nope. I go for something more instinctual. I want God to fix it. Right now.

In this lesson, we continue examining Job's story and his responses to the suffering inflicted upon him. Job 2:7 tells us, "The Adversary departed from the LORD's presence and struck Job with severe sores from the sole of his foot to the top of his head." What did Job do? What would you do?

De-fault Theology

Many of the examples I use in this series of lessons from Job may seem to suggest that I might assume God is at least partially responsible for the bad things we go through. I don't actually believe that. I do believe that God is the source of all that is good and is in opposition to evil. The God of love would never bring misery and sickness and evil down on the head of anyone, much less someone who believes in God.

But then, in moments of suffering, all that fine theology has a tendency to slip out of my head. Then, all I want is an all-powerful God who hears my cries and says, "Whoops! Didn't mean to hit you with that tragedy that I sent down. My bad! Let me clean that right up for you!" I want to be able to lay all the blame at God's feet. I want a God I can yell at and demand justice from. I want a God I can fault for all that is wrong with the world.

Job's story is interesting because it sets up this quandary. Job didn't know that Satan and God were involved together in a plan to see if Job would blaspheme. But we know. While we know it was Satan who did the actual ill to Job, it sure looks like God was at the very least complicit. The frame of the book fits this theology that many of us say we do not have.

In Job 1:21–2:10, Job is not yet deeply wrestling with God. Job is, however, naming God in the struggles he faces. Remember, at this point, Job has already lost his livestock, his workers, and his children. But here he sounds as if he is lifting a prayer or singing a hymn of praise: "The LORD has given; the LORD has taken; bless the LORD's name."

In this moment, Job credited God with what was happening to him. It was God who had afflicted him, as far as Job was concerned. Job was de-faulting himself, no-faulting the Adversary (who, as far as Job knew, was not even part of the equation), and defaulting to a theology that faults God for all that happens in the world.

Our faith tradition does not put the blame on God for evil. We know that it is a product of free will to make our own choices. We know that we have broken the world with our sin. We know that, ultimately, we have a responsibility to seek restoration of our relationship with God so that we can cooperate with God's saving work.

But there are many days when I don't want to cooperate. I want God to swoop in and clean the slate. I fail to see that means some of the chalk would have to be erased from me, too. Those days, I fall to my own de-fault theology, too.

When have you wanted to blame God for things going wrong in your life?

A Biblical Conversation

Pinning down who God is, even if we limit ourselves only to the Scriptures and don't take into account our own histories and experiences of God, is practically impossible. Job stands in tension with a dominant theology of other biblical witnesses, particularly Deuteronomy. Deuteronomy roughly spells out a theology that celebrates the idea that, if you do good, you will be rewarded by God with a good life. If you do bad, however, you will receive punishment.

When I was in seminary, we boiled down Deuteronomistic theology to "do good, get good; do bad, get bad (abbreviated DGGG, DBGB). That is a lovely theology, except it is not true, at least not all the time. It's true that sometimes good people are rewarded. But sometimes some of the most despicable people on the planet seem to gain more and more and more, and some dear saints just continue to suffer.

It is into that reality that Job stepped. Job's story points out that sometimes righteous people suffer, too.

Now, we can debate how righteous Job was. Actually, we can't debate how righteous Job was, and that may be the problem. We are told that he was "honest, a person of absolute integrity; he feared God and avoided evil" (Job 1:1).

We are also given enough other details to see that Job is set up as the ideal proof of DGGG theology. He was wealthy. He had lots of children. He had many servants. He also made sacrifices and performed acts of purification on behalf of his children, just to try to cover them in case they had sinned in their hearts. Job is the poster boy for DGGG theology. Here was a practically perfect man. Was he too perfect to be realistic?

In affliction, Job behaved like a lot of us would behave in such states. He whined and moaned, sank into depression, and became furiously angry. Despite the prevalence of the saying to the contrary, he certainly did not just patiently sit by and receive whatever came at him. Job moved from being a caricature of perfection, which he is still holding onto in the text for this lesson, to being a real person with real pain and loss. In that space, the gloves tend to come off. Eventually.

When have you seen "do good, get good" theology fail?

The Problem of Evil

All of this is driving at the problem of evil. Where does evil come from?

Let's acknowledge that the answer to this question will be one we will wrestle with not only throughout this lesson, but throughout our lives. The answer will feel like a moving target. In this passage alone, we seem to have at least two answers.

Job credited God, but we know that the Adversary was actually inflicting the pain. Then, as we pull back and look at the whole, it also feels as if humanity had a role to play here, too. After all, Job's friends were not terribly helpful in this moment. In fact, they often added to his pain. So don't we sometimes participate and even create brokenness in the world, too?

This is a long-wrestled theological problem. Add to that the challenge that we are coming at it from our limited human perspective, something God will call out at the end of this book (spoiler alert). Big moments such as the Holocaust; the Indonesian tsunami the day after Christmas 2004; or the smaller but more personal struggle in my home state of Arkansas, which got riddled with tornadoes in the midst of a pandemic—those events will cause us to reflect on the nature of evil.

But so will sitting with someone who has lost a child to cancer, comforting a widower whose young wife was killed by a drunk driver, or trying to find purpose and focus after going through a school shooting. Whether on a large communal or nationwide scale or a catastrophic event at a personal level, sooner or later everyone has to ask where evil comes from because it is staring them in the face. Then we want to demand answers.

Job's wife was already there. "Are you still clinging to your integrity?" she asked Job. "Curse God, and die" (Job 2:9). Job wasn't there—yet. He would get right up to that door and knock. But can we blame him?

If this is the way God runs things, then what good is there in following and supporting this God? But if we take a deep breath and step back, if we re-center ourselves on what we actually believe, if we remember who God is to us, then we can trust God again. Right?

How do you explain where evil comes from?

Do You Trust Me?

In the animated movie *Aladdin*, Princess Jasmine and Aladdin are pursued by Jafar's henchmen. Aladdin leans over and asks Jasmine, "Do you trust me?" She says yes, and they jump off a building together. Later, when Aladdin is disguised as Prince Ali and he is offering to show her the world on a magic carpet, he leans over again and asks, "Do you trust me?" Again, Jasmine says yes.[1]

But let's think about what is happening there. Aladdin is lying to Jasmine about who he is when he is Ali, and he is still inviting her to trust him. She will learn the truth eventually, and because it is a Disney cartoon, all will be forgiven. But in reality, that kind of deception would make someone seriously question whether such trust should be extended again.

Now let's consider another movie with the same line. In *Titanic*, Jack invites Rose to stand on the bow of the ship, to spread her arms, and to fly as he did in an earlier scene where he declared himself the king of the world. He asks Rose to step up, and when he does, he asks, "Do you trust me?" She does. He keeps her secure as she ventures beyond her comfort zone. But that is not all Jack does.[2]

At the end of the movie, Jack makes sure Rose is safe on the debris and gives his own life keeping her from harm. He has proven himself wholly trustworthy.

The God we encounter in Job is the God of all creation. This God is the God of things far beyond our comprehension, which we will see as the Book of Job draws to a close. There is much about this God that is beyond us. We are invited, then, to trust that God.

We don't have a whole lot to go on for that trust. From Job's perspective, yes, it appears that God had historically blessed him with abundance. God had been Job's protector and provider, at least as Job understood it, and as he still understands it in this passage (though he will talk himself out of that understanding as the story goes on). God had been trustworthy up to that point. Why should Job question that now?

From our perspective, though, we see a God who is willing to allow lives to be put at risk to prove a point to Satan. Sure, Job's life was protected, but what about the lives of his children? Were they expendable just to make an illustration?

Our view of God through this story is different than the limited view Job had at this moment. But then, our view is all we have in Scripture anyway. We can only encounter the Scripture that we can comprehend. We can't understand beyond our capacity, and God will always be beyond our capacity. Accepting that is how we come to terms with allowing God to be God.

However, this is not the only Scripture passage we have. In addition to the plural witnesses to God mentioned above, we also have the Gospels. Those Scriptures reveal a God who is willing to live the way we live, to feel the way we feel, to suffer and die the way we suffer and die, all in the name of drawing us closer to our own full and abundant salvation.

We have Jesus, the one who will give of himself to protect all of us. Do we trust God? Yes. We trust God because God is God, but we also trust God because God is Jesus.

What helps you trust God?

Mighty Lord, we know we cannot possibly comprehend how you are working in our lives and our world. Help us, even in the midst of such uncertainty, to continue to trust in you; in Jesus' name we pray. Amen.

[1]From *Aladin* (Walt Disney Pictures, 1992).
[2]From *Titantic* (Paramount Pictures, 1997).

Focal Passage: Job 19:1-6, 13-19
Background Texts: Job 19:1-27; Psalm 43:1-5
Purpose Statement: To refuse to be content with letting injustices continue unimpeded

Job 19:1-6, 13-19
¹Then Job responded:
²How long will you harass me
   and crush me with words?
³These ten times you've humiliated me;
   shamelessly you insult me.
⁴Have I really gone astray?
   If so, my error remains hidden inside me.
⁵If you look down on me
     and use my disgrace to criticize me,
⁶   know then that God has wronged me
   and enclosed his net over me.
He has distanced my family from me;
   my acquaintances are also alienated from me. . . .
¹⁴My visitors have ceased;
   those who know me have forgotten me.
¹⁵My guests and female servants think me a stranger;
   I'm a foreigner in their sight.
¹⁶I call my servant, and he doesn't answer;
   I myself must beg him.
¹⁷My breath stinks to my wife;
   I am odious to my children.

¹⁸Even the young despise me;
  I get up, and they rail against me.
¹⁹All my closest friends despise me;
  the ones I have loved turn against me.

Key Verses: "If you look down on me and use my disgrace to criticize me, know then that God has wronged me and enclosed his net over me" (Job 19:5-6).

Three years. It took three years for us to make it to trial. My dad had been fired from a company he had worked with for 21 years. He had seen it coming, though. He had suspected it was coming when he hired the first two black employees to work for the company in its history other than as janitors and lawn care workers.

He had consulted an attorney ahead of his firing who told him he could make copies of anything he wanted and take those copies home; but as soon as he was fired, he would not be able to touch anything. So he had amassed a room full of evidence, evidence that proved discrimination and proved that he was good at his job and was unjustly fired. His goal in going to court, though, was to right the wrongs of injustice.

He wanted this company he loved and had poured more than two decades of life into to live more fully into its own ideas of service and hospitality. Three years, though. Three years is a long time to wait for justice. It took a deep toll on our family economically, emotionally, and spiritually. By the time the trial came, my dad was still single-minded. He was still focused on changing an unjust system. The rest of us in the family, though, were just angry.

Seeking justice in this world is not easy. We encounter a need for justice when our lives seem unfairly turned upside down. But that understanding of justice equates justice with fairness and also assumes justice is all about us. But is that a just approach to justice?

Going on Strike

"I am going on strike from life lessons," I announced to my mother. It was one of those periods of life when too many challenges stacked on top of each other. I decided that, if God or the universe was trying to teach me lessons by making me go through such hard things, then I would just refuse to learn the lessons, so there would no longer be a point to the hard things. Then whatever force was doing this to me could just quit.

At the time of this writing, strikes and protests are underway all around. We are in the midst of the Covid-19 quarantine. In the course of these few weeks, medical professionals have stood with signs outside hospitals, drawing attention to the fact that they need masks and gloves so they can do their jobs safely. Online retail workers are protesting that they continue to send out nonessential items. And people who are tired of staying home are marching in the streets to reclaim their movement, even potentially at the cost of their own health and safety.

When our worlds turn upside down, we would do just about anything to turn them right side up. We long for what is known, for what is comfortable. However, sometimes our comfort depends on someone else's misery.

It is only when we find ourselves in miserable states as well that we see how messed up the world is. It is only when we are inconvenienced, afflicted, or oppressed that we have a greater understanding of what others in similar circumstances face.

Still, we have to be open to seeing those similarities. We have to decide if we are going to choose to strike to make the world different and better, or if we are going to strike against that possibility by staying in our own selfish perspective. It is the choice between self-pity and transformation. Both journeys, though, are often motivated by something unjust. Our response is what makes the difference.

What is your typical reaction to experiencing an unjust situation?

Just Say No

During this Covid-19 pandemic, another place that people have raised objections is on social media. Some of them are disguised in humor, particularly in the myriad of memes that were passed around. Some examples of humorous but frustrated, angry, or biting words included:

- Your screen time last week: six years.
- When someone in your house comes back from getting groceries: "What's the news of the outside world? Tell me everything!"
- We all spent years making 20/20 vision jokes, but none of us saw this coming.
- You wanted weekends to last longer; now here we are.
- Whoever is supposed to go to Nineveh, just GO ALREADY!

Those are all words that express, through humor, the challenge of those days. But sometimes the words are not softened by humor. Sometimes we need to pour out exactly what we mean without any sugar-coating to it at all.

Job's words began to get more insistent, more bitter, and closer to blasphemy. He did not out and out deny God, but he started laying blame for how he was suffering at God's feet. "How long will you harass me and crush me with words?" he asked (Job 19:2).

Job was also getting pretty tired of the perspective his friends were bringing, and he voiced how disillusioned he was with his relationship with his wife: "My breath stinks to my wife," he said (verse 17). Everything was starting to come crashing down, and with good reason! He had lost children, house, home, wealth, and health. Who wouldn't feel cursed—and feel like cursing—in such a moment?

Periodically, people will talk about how they know they shouldn't be angry. I hear this often from people of faith who think that to be "good Christians," they must be content all the time. But people go through some ridiculously hard and unjust things in the course of their lives.

Faith does not make us bulletproof from life's onslaught. We are created in the image of God, and Scripture affirms that God gets angry. In particular, God gets angry over unjust suffering.

If we never voiced our anger about injustice, no one would know there was a need for change. Speaking out about problems, afflictions, and oppressions is the motivation for doing something about them. If we don't know, then we can't say, "No!"

Lament that comes honestly from frustrations about situations that seem undeserved and unfair is an important expression of our faith. Righteous anger has a place in our faith. Such anger is often the fire that fuels the breaking in of the reign of God.

When have your angry words helped motivate change for good?

Obstruction of Justice

It is perhaps no coincidence that Job began in the court of the Lord. The text doesn't explicitly say that, but the divine beings have brought themselves before the Lord. As we noted in an earlier lesson, the Adversary here is the equivalent of a heavenly prosecuting attorney. Is it any wonder that questions of justice become so prevalent here?

Obstruction of justice describes the crime of willfully interfering with the process of justice particularly by influencing, threatening, harming, or impeding a witness, juror, or legal officer, or by furnishing false information in or otherwise impeding an investigation or legal process. Certainly, in Job's case it seems like justice was being interfered with. The obstruction was perpetrated, even, by an officer of the court so to speak (the Adversary). But the judge God was at the very least complicit in the work of the Adversary.

It feels impossible to see how justice can occur here because the justice system was stacked against Job. That is why it is understandable that Job danced right up on the edge of blasphemy. If there was ever a reason to stop revering God, it seems like making you the wager in a bet and leveling you as part of that bet is the best reason there is.

Of course, as far as the narrative goes, Job did not know about the arrangement between God and the Adversary. Still, from Job's perspective, and his apparent theological commitment, God had just decided to beat Job down.

So was God obstructing justice? Was God threatening or harming a witness? What is the witness Job provided? Job was witnessing to God's power and presence in his life. Technically, Job was still witnessing to that reality. Job may have been angry with God for the way he had been treated, but Job had not denied God. Because Job continued to witness to God's power, justice was not being obstructed. Why? To understand that claim, we need to think about what actually constitutes justice.

When have you experienced an interference in justice?

Brought to Justice

What is justice? Again, we find ourselves at a philosophical question for which there are a multitude of answers. There are big answers and personal answers to this question, as my family learned in the course of our long lawsuit.

We finally made it to trial in January 1998, three years after my dad was fired. What happened? Four intense days of trial, and then the other side came to my dad with a settlement offer. Dad's lawyers were tired. His family was angry. The other side was threatening to drag this out in appeals until my dad was dead. In the midst of weighing his options, my father recognized that he had exposed the evil. He took the settlement.

Within a few years, the leadership of the company turned over. The people who had supervised my father had to answer for their behavior, and they were fairly soon ushered out after the trial. People my father had trained were moved into those positions of leadership. The culture changed. More opportunities were opened for more people.

But for us? My father's lawyers were paid. My dad had enough money to pay off the house and go to school to become a truck driver. He would no longer be in sales or hold an executive position. Then he would spend just a few years in retirement before dying of cancer that rapidly overwhelmed his body. My mom lives in their house and manages on social security.

Did we get justice? Yes and no. Yes, things changed for the better—for other people. Not as much for us. Thinking about that experience inspires reflection on Job. Was Job's experience just? Yes and no. Job didn't deserve the suffering he went through, but then many people don't deserve what they go through. But Job witnessed to the power of God in his life.

Job has also given all of us permission to name injustice, to level charges. The justice of the Book of Job, then, is larger than the experience of one man. The justice of Job is to show us that justice can always be sought. In fact, justice can always be demanded.

In 2008, a movie came out entitled *God on Trial*, in which a group of Jews facing death at the Auschwitz concentration camp hold a rabbinic court to see if God is the source of their misery. The movie dramatically illustrates debates that were likely going through the minds of most of the people in the Nazi death camps.

How could a just God allow this to happen? Again, the question of evil gets tangled up in that answer. The point in this moment, though, is that people have permission to ask that question. The Book of Job gives voice to those exact questions. So when we think about defining biblical justice, we need to recognize that our understanding of justice without this book would not be nearly as deep.

Was what happened to Job fair? No. Justice isn't about fair, though. Justice is far more complex than fairness. Justice encompasses the whole of human history. Justice engages systems and breaks the back of evil, eventually. Justice will happen for individuals. But justice is also an umbrella of all that is, which means that, as long as we live in a broken world, some will be treated unjustly as we bend the arc of history toward justice.

Finally, what is justice? Well, from our faith perspective, justice comes from God. In that sense, justice is whatever God decides is just. That is not a terribly comforting statement when we are on the receiving end of what feels like injustice. There is a bigger picture at work, though. A far more complex unfolding of God's reality of human history. We will sometimes pay the price, but hopefully that sacrifice will draw us closer to the reign of God.

No matter what we face, though, we can be confident of two things: We can always challenge injustice, no matter its source. And as we will see in the next couple of lessons, God will always be with us.

What injustice do you want to bring before the court of God?

Lord of justice, give us the words and the courage to name what is wrong and to fight for what is right; in Jesus' name we pray. Amen.

Focal Passage: Job 30:16-23
Background Texts: Job 30:1-31; Psalm 44:9-26
Purpose Statement: To question why God sometimes seems unresponsive to our plight

Job 30:16-23

¹⁶Now my life is poured out on me;
   days of misery have seized me.
¹⁷At night he bores my bones;
   my gnawing pain won't rest.
¹⁸With great force he grasps my clothing;
   it binds me like the neck of my shirt.
¹⁹He hurls me into mud;
   I'm a cliché, like dust and ashes.
²⁰I cry to you, and you don't answer;
   I stand up, but you just look at me.
²¹You are cruel to me,
   attack me with the strength of your hand.
²²You lift me to the wind and make me ride;
   you melt me in its roar.
²³I know you will return me to death,
   the house appointed for all the living.

Key Verse: "Now my life is poured out on me; days of misery have seized me" (Job 30:16).

On a retreat, we had gathered to engage in *lectio divina*, the spiritual practice where someone leads you through intentional contemplative reflection on a passage of Scripture. That morning, we were working with the raising of Lazarus in John 11.

As the guide invited us to see ourselves in the story, I could clearly see who I was. I was Lazarus's mother. You may be wondering where she is mentioned in the story. She is not. In all likelihood, she had probably already died. Despite that, I could see myself as her as clear as the day is long (and at this time, we are in quarantine, so the days are long).

At that time in my life, my son was in trouble. I was worried that the ramifications of the path he was on would lead to death, at least spiritually. There was also deep division between the two of us. So, as I envisioned myself in that scene, I felt as though I was beating the rock covering the tomb, screaming for all I was worth, smashing my arms so hard against the rock they were bloody and bruised, desperate to reach my child.

I didn't even notice as Jesus approached and talked to Martha and Mary. My focus was fully on the tomb and my own rage and anguish. So when Jesus finally made his way to the tomb, he stood right beside me. He looked at the rock, and then he looked at me. Then he touched my shoulder, and he said. . . .

Most of us have had moments in our lives when we thought things could not get any worse. When those times occur, we are desperate for God to hear us. But what if God seems silent? That's where we find Job in the text for this lesson. "Days of misery have seized me," he said (Job 30:16). "I cry to you," he said to God, "and you don't answer" (verse 20).

Where is God when we cry out from the depths of our souls?

The Dark Night of the Soul

If you have ever been through a significant struggle in life or felt that your faith was slipping away and you had nothing left to stand on, that God seemed not to exist or had decided to ignore you completely, you have been in a "dark night of the soul." This descriptive phrase is attributed to the 16th-century Spanish Roman Catholic mystic Saint John of the Cross and refers to a spiritual crisis. It is a place of anguish. A place of fatigue. A place of hopelessness. It can be a place where we can get very, very lost.

I suppose there are people who have walked through life with a constant sense of God being present with them. I envy that assurance. I don't doubt the existence of God, primarily because I have encountered God. But I have wondered on occasion about my devotion to God.

Life can be hard, and—right or not—it is very human to think that membership "in the club" ought to bring some privileges. When it comes to faith, it is perfectly natural to think some of those privileges ought to be a life relatively free from trouble. Oh, sure, we can expect the occasional situation that knocks the knees out from under us. That just keeps our attention. But, seriously, God? Can't we get some bulletproof vests here?

But as long as we live in a broken world, a world that is not the reign of God (even if we get regular glimpses), we are not immune from problems, unfairness, or misery. Critical to surviving the dark night of the soul is having people with whom we can share our experiences. We all need those friends who let us drop our filters. Hopefully, those friends are more helpful than Job's.

Still, one thing that was helpful about Job's friends is that they represented different responses to his plight. In this case, they likely represented different theological explanations to suffering. But when we are in a dark night of the soul, we need different friends who bring a unique presence to help us get through.

When I was struggling with the situation involving my son, I went to several people who were ordained with me. In fact, we started a text thread that actually continues to this day and is a space where all of us can bring our worries to one another.

We have each taken a turn at being Job, and we have each taken turns at being the friends. Some of us have even played the role of Job's friend Eliphaz, pointing out when we are getting too mired in self-pity. Even when it feels as if God isn't listening, the family of God still is.

If you find yourself in a "dark night of the soul," who can you call on to walk that path with you?

"I'm a Cliché"

Sometimes the CEB translation strikes me. For example, Job says of God, "He hurls me into mud; I'm a cliché, like dust and ashes" (Job 30:19). *Cliché* doesn't sound like a Hebrew word. Of course, it isn't a Hebrew word; it is an English translation of a Hebrew word. But it is an unusual English word to use in translating a Hebrew word.

The Hebrew word is *wa-et-massel*, the verb form of which turns the meaning of that word into something roughly equivalent to "And I am a proverb." There is a certain logic, then, in translating that phrase as "I am a cliché." It captures the idea that Job felt as though his situation was so over-the-top as to be representative of the worst of human suffering. It is as if someone designed an example for all that can go wrong at once, and Job found himself representing that very reality.

Of course, there is deep dramatic irony here because the Adversary actually did design this moment to do exactly that: test the limits of human suffering. Job was, in fact, the suffering cliché.

A *cliché* is defined as a phrase or an opinion that seems overused and unoriginal, or even a person or thing that seems unoriginal or predictable. It is stereotypical because it is so common in thought or existence. Job had at one time felt as though he was special, even beloved by God. Now he felt debased and common. He felt as if he was ignored, and he had definitely lost the prior sense of privilege he once enjoyed.

Yes, on one level what he was going through was unique to him. On another, though, it was a predictable reality of being human. We all go through periods of painful loss.

We have a number of phrases that captures a similar concept, of feeling as if we are caught in a stereotypical moment, like when we say we are trapped in a bad dream. Bad dreams are almost universal human experiences. That expression is itself a cliché that captures that human condition. There is a reason clichés are clichés, though. They describe something that is familiar to enough people to be used as an expression over and over and over again.

Job probably did feel like a cliché here. We can also say, however, that Job has become a cliché. Whenever we are suffering, we often compare ourselves to Job. Some of those comparisons are warranted. Some of them, such as when we feel "afflicted" because the store is out of our favorite kind of ice cream at the end of a mediocre day at work, maybe not so much.

Still, Job has become representative of suffering. And if there is one thing about suffering, it is a universal human experience. Of course, that is so cliché.

When have you felt like a cliché?

Honest Prayer

I like to listen to music while I write. I have playlists that are built around moods. I choose a list based around the kind of writing I am doing. For writing on Job, I have seesawed back and forth between lists entitled "Angry Thoughtful" and "Contemplative." I have deliberately avoided the lists "Good Times, Good Songs" and "Inspiration."

So as I sit listening to "Contemplative," the Garth Brooks song "Unanswered Prayers" has rolled up. It tells the story of a man who prayed that God would put him together with a high school flame, but that didn't happen. When he ran into that woman years later and imagined what life would be like with her as opposed to life with his wife, he was grateful that God didn't listen to him.

Most of us have probably prayed for something that didn't happen and then been grateful for that. We have probably also prayed for something that didn't happen and we still want it anyway. We fail to see why God didn't respond. We have thought through this, and clearly we have wisdom about what is best for our lives, and we are mystified why God would not just take our word for it. Or we at the very least feel as though we are entitled to an answer.

But is the purpose of prayer transactional? In other words, should we come to God with a list of demands (or to put it more nicely, "requests") and then expect that our faith entitles us to a response?

I have been asked three times to help with confirmation, and all three times I've been responsible for the lesson on the vows of membership. The first thing we vow is how we will support the local church through our prayers.

I tend to ask the confirmands, "What should we not pray to God for?" One young man said, "An Xbox." I responded by telling him to go ahead and pray for that but not necessarily to expect that prayer would be answered. The point, though, is to bring what is on our hearts before God. We should be unfiltered in what we want to bring before God. We should bring our desires, our pains, our angers, our joys—the whole of our human experience. In a sense, it is one of the ways we are a holy and living sacrifice, because we give it all over to God.

For some reason, though, we struggle with bringing ourselves honestly before God. Do we think we can hide something from God? We can't. But maybe bringing things to God makes them too real for us, too. Still, the biblical witness models this for us through lament. Not only in Lamentations, not only in Psalms, but also in these words of Job.

Job finally started taking off the gloves. He called God out for dragging him around and for being cruel. "At night he bores my bones; my gnawing pain won't rest. With great force he grasps my clothing; . . . He hurls me into mud; . . . You are cruel to me, attack me with the strength of your hand" (Job 30:17-18; 19; 21). Job lost his comfortable theology and got real, and it is in that space that God has real invitation to show up.

When have you felt as if you were the most honest with God in your prayers?

Kill the Noise

"Woman, hush."

That was the response Jesus gave me as I found myself before the tomb in the *lectio divina* practice. My reaction? At first, I wanted to object to the order to be quiet. Who was this man to tell me, an aching and heartbroken mother, to hush? But then I saw the man, and something told me not to object, but just to do exactly as he said. So I stood next to him, quietly, while he called my child from the tomb.

I realized in that moment that Jesus was working on my child, but that it was a longer journey than I was giving credit for. Bringing someone from death to life can take awhile. We focus on how quickly Lazarus and Jesus were raised, but I suppose those days of death felt like the longest days on the planet. And they were probably days filled with wailing and moaning, too. Those are necessary pieces of grief. They are necessary pieces of lament.

But it is important also to remember that, yes, God is in the whirlwind, as we will see in the next few chapters of Job. But Elijah's experience in 1 Kings 19:12 was that God is in the thin and quiet, the silence.

I wonder if we don't sometimes miss that God is responding to our cries because we don't stop all our noise and listen. In times of chaos, there is often a lot of noise. It is hard to tamp it down. But a God of real presence like we worship is also found in the most surprising places, speaking in the most surprising ways. But how can we hear if we don't listen? How can we notice the whisper if we won't hush?

Funny enough, I finished writing this lesson as another song rolled up in my song list. This time it is a song by Barlow Girl called "Never Alone." It is a song that affirms that, even when we feel as if God cannot hear us, we are still never alone. But it does so still with an edge and an anguish about affirming that truth, even as God still is silent.

Maybe I should turn off this song list and listen for God. Or maybe I should stop everything, quiet my mind for a minute, and recognize that God is speaking through it, telling me exactly what I need to hear.

When do you hear God most clearly, in the noise or in the quiet?

Lord, when we cry out, help us hear you; in Jesus' name we pray. Amen.

Focal Passages: Job 40:1-5; 41:1-10; 42:1-6
Background Texts: Job 40:1–42:6; Psalm 13:1-6
Purpose Statement: To learn to live faithfully without knowing all the answers

Job 40:1-5
¹The LORD continued to respond to Job:
²Will the one who disputes with the Almighty correct him?
  God's instructor must answer him.
³Job responded to the LORD:
⁴Look, I'm of little worth. What can I answer you?
  I'll put my hand over my mouth.
⁵I have spoken once, I won't answer;
  twice, I won't do it again.

Job 41:1-10
¹Can you draw out Leviathan with a hook,
  restrain his tongue with a rope?
²Can you put a cord through his nose,
  pierce his jaw with a barb?
³Will he beg you at length
  or speak gentle words to you?
⁴Will he make a pact with you
  so that you will take him as a permanent slave?
⁵Can you play with him like a bird,
  put a leash on him for your girls?

⁶Will merchants sell him;
   will they divide him among traders?
⁷Can you fill his hide with darts,
   his head with a fishing spear?
⁸Should you lay your hand on him,
   you would never remember the battle.
⁹Such hopes would be delusional;
   surely the sight of him makes one stumble.
¹⁰Nobody is fierce enough to rouse him;
   who then can stand before me?

Job 42:1-6

¹Job answered the LORD:
²I know you can do anything;
   no plan of yours can be opposed successfully.
³You said, "Who is this darkening counsel without knowledge?"
   I have indeed spoken about things I didn't understand,
   wonders beyond my comprehension.
⁴You said, "Listen and I will speak;
   I will question you and you will inform me."
⁵My ears had heard about you,
   but now my eyes have seen you.
⁶Therefore, I relent and find comfort
   on dust and ashes.

Key Verse: "You said, 'Who is this darkening counsel without knowledge?' I have indeed spoken about things I didn't understand, wonders beyond my comprehension" (Job 42:3).

At the height of its collection, the Library at Alexandria, Egypt, may have held 400,000 works. Now, admittedly, in comparison to the 16 million+ books and 120 million+ additional works in the US Library of Congress, that is a paltry amount. For antiquity, however, the Library at Alexandria represented the greatest repository of human knowledge the world had ever known.

Alexandria itself was a busy port, a meeting place of many of the world's cultures. At times in its history, Alexandria enforced a policy that if you docked and were carrying any written material, you had to surrender it to be copied. It could be returned once scribes had captured it.

It reached its height in the third and second centuries BC. Then, the library began to decline. It lost funding, intellectuals were cast out of Alexandria, and it suffered a series of fires that also destroyed its branch campus at the Serapeum. By the end of the fourth century, the Library at Alexandria was no more.

But what if it had survived? What if it had even thrived? What if it collected and then shared more and more and more of the world's knowledge? Would the so-called Dark Ages have happened? Where would human knowledge be now? What did we know then that would have changed what we know now? If the Library at Alexandria had not been destroyed, would the knowledge contained there have altered the course of history? Then again, are there important limits to our knowledge? Perhaps it is better that we don't know.

Despite the fact that Ecclesiastes warns us, "In much wisdom is much aggravation; the more knowledge, the more pain" (Ecclesiastes 1:18), humans endlessly seek to know. That curiosity can be one of the great virtues of being human and can reflect how we are created in the image of God. But we are the image of God; we are not God. We will come up against limits to what we know, and one of those limits is fully knowing God. That doesn't mean we won't keep trying, though.

Scripture, Tradition, Reason, Experience

As Albert C. Outler studied the works of John Wesley, he noticed that Wesley used four lenses in trying to understand God: Scripture, tradition, reason, and experience. He termed these collective lenses "the Wesleyan Quadrilateral." Basically, the idea behind Outler's model is that Wesley did not just rely on one of these when it came to discerning who God is and what God's will is for us, but instead kept all four approaches in conversation with one another.

While he acknowledged that Scripture is our primary source for knowing God, we also understand God through the study of church and church history in tradition. We use our God-given capacity for reason to reflect on God. We also continue to have individual and collective experiences of God that reveal more of God, too.

Those four lenses are fairly comprehensive. They take into account a full picture of how we can know. The study of how we know, by the way, is called epistemology. The epistemology of the Methodist tradition is in the Wesleyan Quadrilateral. We use a conversation among Scripture, tradition, reason, and experience to know how we respond as people of faith. We also use all four to better understand God. But they are not totally comprehensive.

In the first place, the lenses are limited by individual capacity. We can only know about our experience, and the experience of others that they choose to share with us. Our intellect, our reason, is defined in part by genetics, part by social location as we grew, part by the educational experiences we have had. Our traditional understanding is shaped by the church tradition we choose to give weight to. And Scripture is affected by translation and interpretation.

We cannot even fully utilize the four lenses. How can we possibly comprehensively apply them to the key object of their study, God? Human understanding is limited because humans are limited.

How do you use the Wesleyan Quadrilateral in the understanding of your faith? Is there one lens you lean on more heavily than the others?

The Great "Because I Said So"

My parents said "Because I said so" more times than I could count. It was a terribly frustrating answer to get. I wanted to know why we had to do things, or couldn't do things, whatever the case may be. I promised that I would never do the same thing to my child.

But then I confronted a two-year-old with endless questions. I could only run down that rabbit hole so long. Eventually, I had to hush him up so we could move on with our day! So, I told him we were doing such and such, "Because I said so." The shame I felt was overshadowed by the relief at not having to answer any more questions!

The questions children bring are usually good questions. They may seem simple to us, but if children don't ask the questions, they cannot learn. When we have time and patience to answer them, we contribute to that growth.

Sometimes, though, we don't have the time to answer them. At other times, they are not ready for the answers.

Sometimes we would need to explain too much background, and they would all lose interest before the question was answered. In some cases, their brains just aren't capable of comprehending the answer they seek. It would be like learning simple addition and then asking for help with a calculus question. They aren't ready. We can't go there. In those cases, giving a short answer is an understandable way of handling things.

God did show up and answer Job's questions about suffering. Well, God sort of answered Job's questions. God basically answered Job with a giant "Because I said so." God explained to Job how he could not possibly have the perspective he needed to understand suffering.

God went through a long litany of divine action in creation, of all that God manages beyond Job's miniscule human existence. There is more than a little bit of sarcasm in God's response to Job, effectively saying at times, "Oh, I forgot that you, Job, were there when I set the foundations of the earth!" which of course, Job wasn't. God distinguished between what the divine knowledge includes and what human brains can possibly comprehend.

We are accustomed to knowing anything we want to know. Not knowing frustrates us. We have especially become accustomed to knowing whatever we want to know in an era when the devices we carry in our purses or back pockets contain access to more information than the librarian in Alexandria could have possibly conceived. It is more than the librarians at the Library of Congress can conceive.

We can know practically anything. But even in these conditions, just because we can know doesn't mean that we should know or even that we have the capacity to know. The knowledge that our human minds have access to cannot be contained anymore in a single lifetime.

And the truth of the matter is, we don't know everything. As I write in the shadow of quarantine, when the world is scrambling to come up with a vaccine to combat a miniscule particle that is wreaking havoc on our world, we have come face-to-face with the limits of our knowledge. How much more are those limits exposed when we come face-to-face with the power of God.

When have you been frustrated because you didn't understand something?

Confronting the Whirlwind

We don't know how tornadoes work. We know more about them than we did when my hometown was hit by one in 1975. In those days, we had just a few minutes of warning that a tornado was upon us. Now we may have hours. In fact, once when I lived in Dallas, we were given days of notice that tornadoes would likely hit. Doppler radar and new technologies have taught us much about how tornadoes form.

That being said, we still do not know why certain conditions give rise to tornadoes one time and those same conditions do not produce even high winds the next time. Then there is the unpredictability when the tornadoes do form. We can make rough estimates about the direction tornadoes will head, but that is still an inexact science.

Sometimes tornadoes stay on the ground for an hour or more. Sometimes they pop down for five minutes and dissipate. For all our study and science, there is still so much we don't comprehend about a phenomenon people confront in our world every single year. This one thing we do know, though. When you come face-to-face with a tornado, it will knock you to your knees. To stand in the path of such power is overwhelming, if not also life altering, to say the least.

It seems wholly appropriate, then, that in this encounter with Job, "The LORD answered Job from the whirlwind" (Job 40:6). God appeared in the whirlwind to effectively say, "You don't understand, and you can't understand." And what was Job's response to such incredible power? "I have indeed spoken about things I didn't understand, wonders beyond my comprehension" (42:3).

There is no other answer to confronting the full reality of God. Job wanted answers. What he got instead was the whirlwind. What he got was God.

What is the most awestruck moment from your life, and how did you detect God's presence in it?

The Ultimate Answer
42.

According to *The Hitchhiker's Guide to the Galaxy*, a science fiction series created by Douglas Adams, the answer to The Ultimate Question about Life, the Universe, and Everything is 42. The answer was calculated by a computer named Deep Thought over the course of 7.5 million years. That answer is not terribly satisfying. It also does not take into account what the question is.

Part of being human, I suppose, is at some point or other asking ourselves what the purpose of life is. It is the "Why am I here?" question that eventually, if fleetingly, crosses most of our minds at least once in our lifetime. It is a question seeking significance. Also, because suffering seems to be a universal experience, most of us also ask at some point, "Why me?"

I had such questions once. I was in the midst of a year dealing with surviving a school shooting. When I found myself in another threatening situation on that same campus less than a year later, the house of cards of coping that I had built around me came crashing down. I also finally got angry with God.

I had all the questions that Job had for God and all the accusations, too. Frustrated, scared, and angry, I demanded in prayer in the middle of a worship service that God show up and explain. Tell me why there is evil in the world. Tell me why good people have to suffer. Tell me!

A few hours later, God did show up.

God did not come in a whirlwind for me. God came as an overwhelming presence of peace. I have never been able to adequately describe that moment. But even now, 20 years since it happened, when I try to explain it, I always get goosebumps. And in the course of time that I found myself in God's presence, God did give me an answer to my question.

"You want to know why there is evil in the world? There is no good answer. But here's what you can do. You can come work for me. Spend your life bringing this kind of peace into the lives of others. Then there will be less evil. There will be less suffering. Come work for me."

It was my call to ministry. It still is my call to ministry. It will always be my call to ministry. It is also the answer to my questions. Not everyone's answer. My answer. My answer is distinct from Job's. Job got an answer that basically put him in his place (Job 40:4-5). I suspect that is what Job ultimately needed. But the words that God spoke to each of us, that is only part of the answer we were given. The unspoken answer was the same for both of us.

God is with us. Always. "My ears had heard about you," Job finally said to God, "but now my eyes have seen you. Therefore I relent and find comfort on dust and ashes" (42:5-6).

Ultimately, that is the most satisfying answer of all. It is all we need. We may not recognize it in the heat of days; but when we experience it, we are humbled, we are silenced, we are awestruck. And we never have to question the existence of God again.

It becomes enough to know that there is a God, a God who loves us enough to walk with us through life. There is a God who loves enough to be whirlwind and whisper, to found the universe and care for the sparrow. There is a God who loves enough to become human, walk beside us, experience pain, and reveal that death is defeated.

There are many answers for why there is evil in the world. Some of them are more helpful than others. None of them does away with evil. None of them is ultimately satisfactory. There are also many answers for the role God plays in good and evil. None of them compares to actually encountering God. And even in those encounters, like for Job, the fullness of God's reality is impossible to comprehend.

We will not know, we cannot know, and that is okay. It's what makes God God and us not. *Who* God is—that is not the answer we need. *That* God is—that is the answer we need. And the rest of that answer, that no matter what, God is with us, is all we ever need to know.

How does knowing God provide all the answers to the questions we have?

Lord of all the universe, great and small, we are forever thankful that you love us and are always with us; in Jesus' name we pray. Amen.

Belong
This fall, our lessons center on the theme "Belong." The writer of the student book lessons is Greg Weeks; the teacher book writer is Clara Welch.

Outside In
Sociologists studying the story of the early church often attribute the growth of the church to the sense of belonging that it offered people in a world where belonging was limited to those with things such as property, high status, and birthright. The lessons in this unit look at the various ways that the Bible makes clear how we belong to God's people, even when we appear to be outsiders. They challenge us to consider where we as human beings insert distinctions that restrict membership within the community of Christ.

Into the Future
After over 2,000 years of existence as an institution, we can easily take for granted that we know what the church is. The lessons in this unit invite us to look at it from the view of the community living into the future. The Greek word for church, *ekklesia*, is not a word that the first members of the church associated with a religious activity. The word signifies the assembly of the people of God. It is instructive to look at how these first members of the church understood the purpose of assembling as a group, how this has shaped our understanding of church, and how reading these texts might renew and expand our understanding.

The Fellowship of the Table
The opening of God's people to Jews and Greeks, men and women, masters and slaves required people previously unaccustomed to eating together to sit down at a common table. When we look at the Gospel narratives, we see Jesus modeling open-table fellowship. The lessons in this unit lead us to look at the significance of the practice of open-table fellowship in the church as a sign of God's shared abundance, ministry of reconciliation, and celebration.

CPSIA information can be obtained
at www.ICGtesting.com
Printed in the USA
LVHW020337090621
689682LV00012B/446